3-

A Guide for Teaching Scuba to Divers with Special Needs

BEST PUBLISHING COMPANY

A Guide for Teaching Scuba to Divers with Special Needs

Frank Degnan

BEST PUBLISHING COMPANY

ISBN: 0-941332-64-0
Library of Congress catalog card number: 97-075325

Composed, printed and bound in the United States of America.

Best Publishing Company
2355 North Steves Boulevard
P.O. Box 30100
Flagstaff, Arizona 86003-0100 USA

Acknowledgments

Throughout the process of writing and producing this book, I have received invaluable support and assistance from a number of people. First and foremost, my wife Debby whose love, patience, and support have been of epic proportions. Next, has to be Carolyn Johnson of Metro Design who has dedicated so many hours to making my jumble of words presentable. In addition, thanks to Mark Medland, also of Metro Design, who dragged Carolyn into this. (However, I am not sure that Carolyn is as thankful to Mark as I am.) Thanks also to my sister Maria who volunteered a great deal of time to proof read the manuscript, and to my brothers Jerome and Greg who provided helpful insights.

Aside from the actual writing of the book, there was also the fun of diving with some great people. My thanks to Corey Anderson, Jeff Jokinen, Mike Leimbach, Ron Leimbach, and Stephen Worden all of whom consented to model for this book. Naturally, for the models to be effective someone has to take some photographs and I am grateful to the photographers, John Nickel and Ed Minard. I am also extremely grateful to Steve Kevin who, over the years, has donated countless hours of lifeguarding so I could have the fun of teaching scuba diving.

I would also like to thank Dr. Nancy Megginson, my thesis advisor, and Dorothy Stonely, friend and Co-Founder of NIADD, for helping motivate me to write this manual.

Unfortunately, it is impossible to name everyone who has assisted me along the way. However I would like to say thank you to the following divers and friends, all of whom have contributed in some way to this work:

Marvin Adams	David McKenney
Charles Blevins	Michael Morrill
Mark Conrad	Michael Morris
Howard Cothern	Rusty Murry
Dyer Crouch	Deanna Priday
Marty Curlee	Dave Quillen
Mark Digiorgio	Jill Robinson
Jim Durand	Paul Rollins
Ken "Keneke" Force	Tim Skelly
A. Dale Fox	Steve Tremblay
Dr. Gatch Gaccione	Bruce Van Hoorn
Patrick Gorman	Stephen Varney
John Heine	Lee Walton
Lenny Hulsebosch	Kathleen Ward
David Houghton	Dr. Conal Wilmot
Dana Johnson	

A special thanks to Frank and Ginny Barry of Any Water Sports Dive Center, for their patience and understanding on all the days I called to say "I won't be at the shop today."

Finally, a great deal of the credit must go to all those divers both past and present who have worked so hard to make scuba and the ocean accessible to us all.

Table of Contents

CHAPTER 3 - Equipment

CHAPTER 6 - Facilities

CHAPTER 7 - Developing Your Program

Introduction

The purpose of this guide is to provide practical information for certified scuba instructors teaching scuba to individuals with special needs. Experienced instructors know that at some point in the training process many students experience difficulties and have some special needs. One student may have had a bad day at work and just need the opportunity to relax for a while before joining the class for the scheduled activities. Another student may have a physical condition which presents some interesting challenges for scuba instruction. Some students just have more difficulty than others and need to proceed at a slower pace, while other students catch on very quickly, and you must find some way to keep them interested while the rest of the class catches up. Successful scuba instructors have developed their own techniques and methods for accommodating the needs of these students. Typically, the techniques and methods developed are based on some combination of personal experience and knowledge shared by other instructors or taken from books and other resources.

This guide will discuss techniques for accommodating the special physical needs of some of your students, with an emphasis on those physical needs which result from spinal cord injury, cerebral palsy, or amputation. While the guide will focus on specific issues related to some specific disabilities, the information is applicable to a wide range of students. For instance, in the section on spinal cord injury, we will discuss osteoporosis; however, osteoporosis can also be a concern for older adults, many of whom are now taking up snorkeling and scuba. In fact, many of your students who benefit from the information in this guide will not appear to have any special needs or disability at all, at least not in the legal or medical sense. Naturally, that raises the question of just what we mean when we say someone has a "disability or "special physical needs."

Certainly there are a number of legal and medical definitions with regard to "physical disabilities." However, the purpose of this manual is to provide practical information, not to split legal and medical hairs. Personally, when it comes to scuba instruction, I am not concerned with definitions as much as I'm concerned with identifying any special needs the student may have and accommodating them safely. Still, it is important to remember that when someone names a specific disability, it will probably have some specific medical or legal significance.

When we think of a person or a diver with a "disability," most of us probably have some concept in mind without actually having a definition of the word. In other words, "you know it when you see it." Or do you? Many people may have disabilities which are not obvious to the rest of us. Other individuals who appear to have very obvious disabilities may not consider themselves to be "disabled" at all. Nevertheless, as you look through this guide or consider accepting someone into scuba training, it might be helpful to have some practical definitions offered by a couple of well recognized training agencies. The Professional Association of Dive Instructors (PADI) considers a disability to be any physical condition which hinders a diver's ability to perform necessary scuba skills. The Handicapped Scuba Association (HSA) feels that any condition that compromises safety while diving can be considered a physical disability.

Ultimately, as you read this guide or as you work with divers with various physical abilities and limitations, you will probably develop your own definition of a "physical disability." Keep in mind, however, that it is important not to stereotype people based on appearance or medical labels.

Another phrase you will encounter in this book is "divers with special physical needs." Personally, I have never seen this phrase used in other literature, much less seen a definition for it. However, with just a little thought, most of us could probably come up with a description of such a diver. My personal concept is that of a diver who, for whatever reason, needs special equipment, requires special accommodation during training, or requires assistance to perform tasks and skills typical of recreational diving. I base this description on the belief that traditional scuba training seeks to produce divers who are capable of performing all standard scuba skills while using conventional scuba gear and without assistance. Furthermore, it seems that these divers are expected to act independently at all times, whether in or out of the water. How many times have you heard the phrase "If you can't carry your own gear, you can't dive?" It is my hope that eventually these attitudes will change.

Personally, I am more concerned with how you handle your gear in the water than how you handle it in the parking lot. Regardless, we must acknowledge that compared to the majority of divers, some divers have special or unique needs which must be accommodated for them to dive in safety and comfort.

Throughout this guide, the phrases "diver with a disability" and "diver with special needs" are used almost interchangeably because, from a practical point of view, we are frequently more concerned with making the necessary accommodations and less concerned with why they are necessary. However, always be aware that some physical or medical issues may be present which dictate what is or isn't an acceptable accommodation. The guide also refers to divers who swim with their upper bodies. This description is applied to divers who have no voluntary control of their legs, and are unable to kick. You will also notice that throughout the guide, both the male and the female gender are used to refer to divers. This is not meant to imply that some skills or roles are more or less appropriate for a particular gender. Instead, it is meant to reflect the fact that scuba diving is a popular activity for both males and females.

Another phrase you will see throughout this guide is "Adapted Scuba Instruction." This refers to instruction or programs which encourage participation by individuals who, for whatever reason, have special needs. Such programs may be limited strictly to divers with special needs, or they may offer classes open to anyone who is interested.

As mentioned earlier, the purpose of this guide is to present information which is both practical and relevant. Furthermore, my objective has been to make the information easy to access and use. Accordingly, the guide has been divided into a number of sections which, when combined, cover the basic information necessary to develop an adapted scuba program or provide instruction to divers with disabilities. However, each section can also be pulled out and used individually. As you read through each section, keep in mind that the information presented may represent just one way to do something. This does not mean that it is the only way, so I encourage you to use these ideas as starting points for your own creativity. Those issues which I consider to be safety issues, particularly those which can be life threatening, are presented in bold type. **However, as the instructor, it is your responsibility to recognize any potential safety issues and take appropriate action.**

In a number of places throughout the guide, photographs have been used to illustrate or support the concepts presented. An interesting point is that while a large number of photographs were taken, many of them did not illustrate a specific point about divers with disabilities or special needs; instead they simply showed a diver taking care of business. Of course, in many ways, that is the most important point of all. Just as each of us in our own way has special needs, once in the water on scuba each of us in our own way is a scuba diver.

As with any scuba instruction, working with students with special needs is fun, challenging and rewarding. Also, just like traditional scuba instruction, adapted scuba instruction can be frustrating. Through it all, just remember that the goal is to assist all students to realize their maximum potential as divers. Be patient, creative and objective, and you will educate safe, comfortable divers who will participate in scuba as a lifelong activity. I am confident that the information presented in this guide will help you achieve this goal.

Chapter 1

Etiquette

CHAPTER OVERVIEW

Experienced scuba instructors know that often how you say or do something is as important as what you actually say or do. When interacting with any student, you must be professional, courteous, friendly and empathetic. At the same time, you must have the respect and confidence of the student. To be successful as an instructor, you must establish an open relationship based on mutual trust and respect between you and the student.

Unfortunately, when first approached by individuals with special needs or physical disabilities, many of us may experience feelings of discomfort, embarrassment, uncertainty, dismay, or even apprehension. Feelings such as these become obstacles to a successful experience for both you and the student. Open Waters, a federally funded national project working to bridge the gap between adapted and traditional scuba training, explained that many individuals with a disability experience feelings of self-consciousness which may be exaggerated if those around them are obviously uncomfortable.

In contrast, some instructors may be overenthusiastic or view individuals with special needs or disabilities as helpless or overly dependent. In their text, _Diving With Disabilities_, Jill Robinson and Dale Fox expressed concern that such instructors may not provide quality instruction. They advised prospective students to avoid instructors who act overbearing or superior.

It seems then that the first, and perhaps the most important, question you must ask yourself is "How comfortable am I with the thought of working with divers with disabilities or special needs?" Fortunately, as a scuba instructor working with divers with special needs you have a number of techniques available to you which make it easier to provide quality training in a comfortable atmosphere.

Creating a comfortable atmosphere when you are interacting with people with disabilities involves learning what I call "etiquette" and what Jill Robinson and Dale Fox described as "Disability Couth." Some of the aspects of etiquette include using proper language, offering assistance in a constructive manner, and not stereotyping people. The bottom line is that we must treat everyone as a valued individual with strengths, weaknesses, and needs. Not surprisingly, this is how I like to be treated and I bet you feel the same way!

ATTITUDE

According to the American National Red Cross, when working in an adapted setting, an instructor must "adequately assess his or her own attitudes and the needs of the student." Such assessment allows for developing an individualized approach to deal effectively with the limitations of you and your students. Along with a number of other experts, the Red Cross has identified a number of elements which are crucial to a positive instructor attitude. These instructor attributes include: creativity, sensitivity, patience, tact, flexibility, initiative, imagination, honesty, empathy, common sense and courage. These characteristics will enable you to look beyond the disability in question and to treat all students as individuals, affording them dignity and respect.

To be successful when working with divers with special needs you must learn to relax and act naturally. For some this will happen easily, while for others it may take time and effort. In her book _Understanding and Accommodating Physical Disabilities_, Dorothy Shrout cautions that some people may require assistance to develop feelings of comfort when work-

---

ing with individuals with disabilities. However, once you have developed a good comfort level with your students you can build an atmosphere of openness and understanding. According to Open Waters, such an atmosphere is crucial to the success of your program.

Many of the instructor characteristics addressed when working in an adapted setting are similar to those called for in traditional scuba instruction. The National Association of Underwater Instructors (NAUI) emphasizes that a scuba instructor must possess an open mind and be sensitive to the needs of all students. NAUI identifies successful instructors as those who are receptive to new ideas and innovations, discarding outdated practices and prejudices in their instruction. NAUI affirms that while some individuals face different limitations, anyone who is physically capable and motivated can learn to dive. The Professional Association of Diving Instructors (PADI) emphasizes that a scuba instructor must not be egotistic and evaluates instructors on attitude and professionalism.

TERMINOLOGY

Another sensitive area for instructors working with divers with disabilities is terminology. The words we use when referring to people with disabilities may influence not only how we feel about them, but how they feel about themselves. For example, words such as invalid or patient create the feeling that the person is ill, even though the majority of individuals with a disability are healthy. As an instructor, you may be reluctant to accept someone into training if you feel that she is ill, but you might be much less uncomfortable if you understood that person simply has some special needs. In fact it seems to me that at some point, virtually every scuba student has some special needs. Sometimes, it is just a simple matter of understanding what those needs are so you can accommodate them.

A number of words and phrases have been identified as creating unfair negative implications for individuals with disabilities. Think about how you feel when you hear words such as cripple, handicapped, invalid, disabled, suffering from, or confined to a wheelchair. As a general guideline, many experts suggest that proper terminology places the individual ahead of the disability. For example, it would be appropriate for you to say "a diver with a disability", but to say "a disabled diver" may be inappropriate, not to say misleading. To me a "disabled diver" is a diver who needs to be rescued, while a "diver with a disability" is a diver who has accommodated a specific disability and developed techniques for diving safely. Language which places the individual ahead of the disability is referred to as "person-first" terminology.

The issue of terminology is complicated, and many individuals with disabilities disagree on appropriate terminology. Practically speaking, perhaps the best thing you can do is to learn and respect the preferences of the individuals around you. It has been my experience that common sense, common courtesy, and honesty will get you through most situations. Also, when speaking with an individual with a disability, don't worry if you use phrases such as "see you later", "listen to this", or "let's run over to the dive shop." These sayings are part of everyday conversation and should not be cause for embarrassment. The words you use are important, but ultimately it is your attitude that counts.

COMMUNICATION

As mentioned earlier, sometimes how you say something is as important as what you say. This is as true when communicating with individuals with disabilities as it is with anyone else.

The next time you are out with someone with a disability, pay attention to the reactions of those around you. Frequently you will find that they attempt to speak to your companion through you. It is probably not intentional, but it is still inappropriate. Without being rude, you should take steps to ensure that your companion is included as an integral part of any conversation. Sometimes this may be as easy as taking care not to answer questions addressed to you but intended for your companion. Instead, pass the question to your companion and allow him or her to answer. Also, your companion should ask any questions which she or he would like to have answered. If you do this consistently, eventually the others involved in the conversation will feel comfortable doing the same thing.

You must always be alert not to get sucked in to the stereotyping actions of others. For example, always identify the person with whom you are really communicating and speak directly to that person even in the presence of an interpreter or companion. Simply by being aware of the ways in which you can help others overcome or avoid these same errors and by demonstrating proper behavior, you will become a role model as well as an advocate for fair treatment of persons with disabilities.

Social rituals can also be a source of confusion or discomfort when you first meet someone with a disability. I have found that I am most comfortable when I don't make an issue of the person's disability. When I first meet someone with a disability, I offer to shake hands as that is the normal social greeting for me. If the person can respond with a handshake they will. If not, they have probably developed some other response which is every bit as appropriate. The trick is for you to be open and receptive. That way, there is no reason for them to be self-conscious. Perhaps Dorothy Shrout, Co-Founder of the National Instructors Association for Divers with Disabilities (NIADD) put it best when she said "It is no secret to a person with a disability that they have a disability".

It is important that you respect the personal space of individuals with disabilities, just as you should with anybody.

Furthermore, you should always handle wheelchairs or other assistive devices with respect and care, as many individuals with disabilities consider these items to be part of their body. I was told the story of one individual who, prior to his bungy jump, had himself belted and duct taped into his chair. As he put it, "This chair is my legs and you can't jump without your legs."

When speaking with a person with a disability, it may be important, or at the very least polite to consider that person's disability. For instance, when conversing with a person seated in a wheelchair, it may be more comfortable to sit down so that everyone is at eye-level.

When communicating with students with speech or hearing impairments, it is important to make sure that both you and the student understand each other. Do not hesitate to ask them to repeat themselves as many times as possible to ensure that complete understanding has been achieved. Likewise, take steps to ensure that they understand you completely. One technique is to phrase questions so that only a short answer is required or even just a shake of the head. In many cases, people may give up due to fear of causing embarrassment, self-consciousness or frustration for everyone involved. However, particularly in a scuba setting, this could create a dangerous situation. Techniques for successful communication include: repeating what you understand and allowing the other person to react, or using body language or written communication. If you are speaking with a deaf person who reads lips, it is important to stand in good light, face the person directly, and speak slowly without food, cigarettes, gum or other objects in your mouth. It is not necessary to exaggerate your speech. Always remember, **it is important not to compromise the quality of communication out of fear of embarrassing yourself or your students.**

OFFERING ASSISTANCE

Another aspect of etiquette involves offering assistance to individuals with disabilities or special needs. Ultimately, the type and amount of assistance given should be determined by the individual accepting assistance. It is important that you always ask the person if they would like some assistance. Do not simply assume that assistance is needed and jump right in. You may cause more harm than help. If the person accepts your offer, ask him to explain what they would like you to do and how he would like you to do it. Keep in mind that the needs and desires of individuals with disabilities are as varied as the individuals themselves.

For you, as a scuba instructor, the question of when and how to offer assistance is one of educational philosophy, and of course, we must consider the safety aspects as well. My personal guideline is to offer assistance in the same manner and for the same reasons or circumstances as I would for any other student. Sometimes however, it is difficult to tell when to step in for safety reasons. It may be that a student with a disability looks like she is struggling when compared to other students, or she may use techniques which are different from those you typically teach. However, that student may actually be operating well within her own personal comfort zone. **As the instructor, you must distinguish between techniques which are unsafe and those which are just different**. Also, you must learn what is a normal level of exertion and when a student is really struggling. In virtually every class I have ever taught, I have seen a wide range of ability and performance among students. Be careful not to jump to conclusions simply because you think a student has a disability or special needs.

CHAPTER SUMMARY

As a scuba instructor working with students with disabilities or special needs, it is crucial that you be comfortable with the idea of teaching them to dive. You must also be comfortable with yourself as well as with your students. Becoming familiar with the etiquette for interacting with people with disabilities will be a great help in developing a good comfort level. Then, you will be able to create the open, trusting atmosphere which is necessary for a successful program. Remember that the qualities you need to be a successful scuba instructor are the same no matter who your students happen to be.

REVIEW OF MAIN POINTS

- Develop an individualized approach to effectively accommodate your limitations as well as those of your students.
- Be aware of and respect the preferences of others with regard to the language and terminology you use. When in doubt, use language which emphasizes the individual not the disability.
- Be a role model by both avoiding stereotypes and helping others to avoid them as well.
- Handle wheelchairs and other assistive devices with respect and care.
- **Don't sacrifice quality of communication out of frustration or fear of embarrassment.**
- Ideally you should always ask before giving assistance and then provide only the assistance necessary. **However, don't sacrifice safety for the sake of being polite.** If the student's safety is at risk, provide immediate assistance, then make sure to explain what you did and why.
- Learn to distinguish between techniques which are unsafe and those which are just different.
- Do not jump to conclusions just because you think a student has a disability or special needs.

APPLYING YOUR KNOWLEDGE

1. Identify three components of etiquette when interacting with individuals with disabilities.
2. As an instructor, describe actions you can take to develop an individualized approach to help overcome your limitations as well as those of your students.
3. According to Open Waters, what elements contribute to an atmosphere which will promote success in your program?
4. Describe person first terminology and how it might be used in a scuba setting.
5. Describe one commonly encountered method of communication which is inappropriate, and how you can correct this behavior.
6. Describe techniques for effectively communicating with individuals with speech or hearing impairments.
7. Discuss appropriate ways to offer assistance. Provide examples which you might use in an actual scuba instruction setting.
8. As a scuba instructor concerned with the safety and success of your student, it is important to intervene in an appropriate manner and at appropriate times. Discuss considerations for doing so.

REFERENCES

American National Red Cross. (1977). Adapted aquatics: Swimming for persons with physical or mental disabilities. Washington, DC: Author.

Carroll, J. F. (1987). Scuba diving with disabilities. Sports 'N Spokes, 13, 45-47.

Council for National Cooperation in Aquatics (1982). Aquatics now. In R. D. Clayton (Ed.), Holiday Inn and the Ohio State University Columbus Ohio Council for National Cooperation in Aquatics (pp. 179-187). Indianapolis, IN: Author.

Emmerson, L., Ravendale, J., Atterbury, S., Isabelle, H., North York Y-Nauts, Toronto Snorkelauts, Carmichael, B., Garrett, G., & Murray, R.. (n.d.). Skin diving for the physically handicapped. (Available from Moray Wheels Adaptive Scuba Association, PO Box 1660 GMF, Boston, MA. 02205)

Green, J. S., & Miles B. H. (1987). Use of mask, fins, snorkel, and scuba equipment in aquatics for the disabled. Palaestra, 3(4), 12-17.

Hanauer, E. (1981). Sea legs. Sports 'N Spokes, 6, 27-30.

Handicapped Scuba Association. (1987). H.S.A. instructor's manual. (Available from Handicapped Scuba Association 1104 El Prado, San Clemente, CA. 92672).

Jankowski, L. W. (1995). Teaching persons with disabilities to scuba diving. (Available from Quebec Underwater Federation / F.Q.A.S. (Fédération Québécoise des Activitiés Subaquatiques) 4545, ave Pierre-De Coubertin, C.P. 1000, succ. M Montréal (Québec) CANADA H1V 3R2.

Lasko-McCarthey, P., & Knopf, K. G. (1992). Adapted physical education for adults with disabilities. Dubuque, IA: Eddie Bowers Publishing, Inc.

Miller, P. D. (ed.). (1995). Fitness programming and physical disability. Champaign,IL: Human Kinetics.

Myers, J. (1995, Fourth Quarter). The challenges of leadership. The Undersea Journal, 4-6.

National Association of Underwater Instructors. (1991). NAUI standards and procedures manual (3rd ed.). (Available from National Association of Underwater Instructors, PO Box 14650, Montclair, CA. USA 91763).

Open Waters (1994). Open waters scuba diving for everyone: A guide to making diving training accessible to people with disabilities. (Available from Open Waters c/o Alpha One, 127 Main St., South Portland, ME 04106).

Professional Association of Dive Instructors. (1993). PADI instructor manual. (Available from Professional Association of Dive Instructors, 1251 East Dyer Rd. #100, Santa Anna, CA. 92705-5605 USA).

Robinson, J., & Fox, A. D. (1987). Scuba diving with disabilities. Champaign, IL: Leisure Press.

Shrout, D. S. (1994). Understanding and accommodating physical disabilities: The manager's desk reference. Westport, CT: Quorum Books.

Wallach, J. (1991, June). Accessible oceans. Rodale's Scuba Diving, 91-96.

Williamson, J. A., McDonald, R. W., Galligan, E. A., Baker, P.G., & Hammond, C. T. D (1984). Selection and training of disabled persons for scuba diving Medical and psychological aspects. The Medical Journal of Australia, 141, 414-418.

Chapter 2

Medical Aspects

CHAPTER OVERVIEW

For many instructors, the most intimidating aspect of training divers with physical disabilities may be medical or health concerns. As scuba instructors, we have all had some exposure to the medical and physiological aspects of scuba diving, and we realize there are some important questions which must be asked of any prospective student. However, most of us aren't familiar with the medical aspects of the various physical disabilities, and there may be issues of which we aren't aware or which are unfamiliar. Therefore, any time there is a question regarding the medical history or status of a prospective student, it is prudent to consult the Divers Alert Network or a physician familiar with diving medicine.

Keep in mind that a person with a disability is not necessarily ill or unfit. In fact, an individual with a physical disability may be a more suitable candidate for scuba than an individual without a "disability" but who has chronic sinus problems, for example.

This section will present some of the medical considerations for training divers with physical disabilities, beginning with some general concerns for screening potential students. The possible implications of spinal cord injury, spastic cerebral palsy, and amputation will be discussed with regard to diving and travel. Information presented will include a brief description of the disability, effects of the disability, and accommodating the special needs of some divers. Practical explanations will be given for some common terms.

SCREENING STUDENTS

One of the most difficult aspects of scuba instruction can be screening prospective students. What makes a person suitable or unsuitable for scuba training? One extreme might be to say that virtually everyone can scuba dive to some extent, even if it means never leaving the shallow end of a swimming pool. The other extreme might claim that only those who can function independently as a diver and handle rough ocean conditions should be considered for scuba training. However, for most scuba instructors, the reality of accepting students into training falls somewhere between the two extremes. The nationally recognized scuba training agencies have established standards, based on some combination of medical and physical criteria, for accepting prospective students into training. However, many students may fall into a "gray area" with regard to water skills, medical or physical condition, or physical ability. These difficulties may become more complicated when considering accepting individuals with physical disabilities into a scuba training program.

Medical Criteria

The issue of medical screening of dive students can be confusing, and a great deal of debate has taken place regarding what is or isn't an absolute contraindication for scuba diving. Chris Wachholz of the Divers Accident Network (DAN) notes that the lack of medical information regarding diving with disabilities makes categorical decisions in this area difficult. He suggests that physicians evaluating prospective divers should consider medical conditions which would increase the risk of drowning, decompression sickness, barotrauma, or loss of consciousness. He also recommends considering the individual's overall health, including any medications currently being taken and the reasons for taking the medication. Furthermore, he expresses concern regarding the potential danger posed to divers as a result of a buddy's physical limitations. Ultimately, a consensus must be reached among the student, the instructor, and the physician. The decision must also fall within the guidelines or standards established by the instructor's certifying agency.

The issue of diving with a disability can be controversial. Some people might not consider disabilities which limit mobility on land to be contraindications to diving. Others might consider the risk to the diver and his or her buddy to be too great, and refuse to approve that person for scuba training. Dr. Charles Brown noted that there are no clearly defined criteria for medical screening of recreational divers. Dr. Brown stated that he would approve a 65 year old student with a physical disability as long as that student had a strong desire to dive, would dive only in favorable conditions, and would partner with a trustworthy dive buddy. At the same time, Dr. Brown noted that many physicians would disagree with him regarding approval of such a candidate for scuba training. The British Sub Aquatic Club requires that any scuba candidate be "medically fit to dive so that his companions do not have to worry about him."

Based on a study conducted in Australia in 1984, Williamson, McDonald, Galligan, Baker and Hammond concluded that proper evaluation of a student with a disability requires knowledge of the individual's rehabilitation process, diving medicine, and common dive practices. However, they also cautioned that results of medical testing of muscular coordination must be interpreted with care, as they may result in the physician's underestimating the prospective student's suitability for training in scuba diving. **Many experienced instructors agree that it would be unwise for an individual to engage in scuba training too soon after an illness or accident, and that no one should be accepted into training until a qualified physician has judged him or her mentally, emotionally and medically fit to dive.** At the same time, they pointed out that scuba training can be beneficial for the physical self-concept of an individual with a disability, and that every effort should be made to make the experience positive and enjoyable.

Physical Ability Criteria

According to the National Oceanic and Atmospheric Administration (NOAA), "Non-physical attributes such as good judgment, a healthy respect for personal, environmental, and equipment limitations, and constant attention to safety are now considered as important, if not more important, to safe recreational diving than physical strength." The _NOAA Diving Manual_ Diving for Science and Technology further states that divers with disabilities employ techniques that "minimize the amount of effort required to accomplish a given task- a clear advantage for any diver."

NOAA does point out that students should posse a high level of comfort in the water and react calmly when confronted with unexpected stress. Prospective students should be evaluated for confidence and competence as well as their ability to "maintain themselves comfortably on the surface of the water for reasonable periods of time, both in a stationary position and while moving through the water for a specified distance. These requirements emphasize stamina rather than speed, skill, or physical force".

When observing prospective students in the water, it is important not to be deceived by appearances. In many instances, what appears uncomfortable to the evaluator, is simply the normal swimming technique for that individual. Be prepared to spend some extra time, and focus on safe effective technique rather than speed or style. Evaluate the student for comfort level, strength, stamina, breathing, range of motion and buoyancy characteristics. Divers with disabilities may exhibit unusual buoyancy characteristics which require unconventional weight distribution.

Depending on the severity of the disability in question, **it may also be appropriate to evaluate the student's ability to perform basic water safety skills such as rolling over from front to back, or standing up in shallow water without assistance.** Also, it is important to evaluate the student's ability to perform these skills both with and without equipment, such as wet suits, which will be used while scuba diving. Some students, who are capable of performing these skills wearing only a bathing suit, may become unable to perform them when working against the stiffness and buoyancy of a wet suit.

SPINAL CORD INJURY

Description

The spinal cord is made up of nerve fibers which allow messages, in the form of nerve impulses, to be sent back and forth between the body and the brain. The cord itself is protected by the vertebrae, which together make up the vertebral column or spine. Typically, an adult will have twenty four individual vertebrae as well as the sacrum and the coccyx, both of which are made up of several vertebrae which have fused together. The vertebrae are typically identified by the region of the spine in which they are located and by their position within that region. The seven cervical vertebrae (C1-C7) are located in the neck area, with C1 at the top of the spine and C7 at the lower end of the cervical region, or neck. The twelve thoracic vertebrae (T1-T12) are located in the thoracic, or chest area, of the body. T1 is found immediately below C7, the lowest of the cervical vertebrae. T12 is found at the bottom of the thoracic area. The five lumbar vertebrae (L1-L5) are located in the lower back region of the body. L1 is located immediately below T12, and L5 is located at the bottom of the lower back area. Immediately below the lumbar vertebrae is the sacrum, which joins with the pelvis. Finally, at the bottom of the spine is the coccyx or tailbone.

The spinal cord is approximately 18 inches long and is about the size of an adult's thumb. It runs without interruption from the brain to the area of the second lumbar vertebrae (L2). At this point, the cord separates into individual nerve fibers or roots, which make up the cauda equina or "horses tail." A total of thirty one pairs of spinal nerves exit from the spine at various points. It is these nerves that carry the impulses necessary for sensation and voluntary control of bodily functions. Unlike most other tissue in the body, spinal nerve cells do not usually recover from serious injury, so the effects of spinal cord injury are typically permanent.

Spinal cord injury refers to a neurological deficit resulting from bruising, crushing, severing or hemorrhaging of the

---

spine. Damage to the spinal cord can also be the result of diseases such as polio, multiple sclerosis, rheumatoid arthritis, etc. These injuries, referred to as lesions, are frequently described as complete or incomplete, as well as by the level of the injury. [Describing an injury as complete suggests a total loss of both sensation and voluntary control of the body functions controlled by nerves which exit the spine below the level of the injury] The person will also experience loss of control of bowel, bladder, and sexual function, as well as muscle movement. Other body functions such as blood pressure, temperature control, heart rate and respiration may also be affected. Incomplete injuries may result in partial loss of sensation or control, or a combination of the effects described previously. An example would be an individual with spinal cord injury resulting in muscle weakness but not complete loss of voluntary muscle control.

Keep in mind that the information above does generalize to some extent. Also be aware that two individuals may experience injury to the spine at the same level, but due to the nature of the injury, the damage to the cord itself may vary. No two injuries are exactly alike. This means that two individuals, both of whom describe their injury as T7 complete, may have different levels of ability. Also, each may experience feelings and sensations that the other doesn't. Furthermore there may be damage to the cord at more than one level, which means that one side of the body will be affected more than the other. An individual with such an injury might describe it as C 6/7.

Another surprise to many of us is that some people with spinal cord injury live with constant pain from their injury. Others may experience pain if the site of the injury is subjected to pressure. It is important to keep this in mind when working with your students.

The following are some general guidelines for the effects of spinal cord injury at different levels. However, as always, the best thing to do when working with an individual with spinal cord injury is to discuss the situation with her and her physician.

The Effects of Spinal Cord Injury at Various Levels

Cervical C1-C7

- C1-C3 The individual will have severe respiratory problems and may require assistance to breathe.
- C4 The individual will be able to use only the neck muscles and the diaphragm.
- C5 Vital capacity will be decreased.
- C5 The individual will have some use of the wrist and may be able to push a wheelchair.
- C6 The individual will have use of wrist extensors and may be able to push a wheelchair.
- C7 The individual will have control of elbow extension, finger extension and finger flexion.
- Generally individuals with injury to the cervical region will not have voluntary movement or sensation in the torso or legs.
- Spinal cord injury in the cervical region will typically result in quadriplegia.

Thoracic T1-T12

- T1-T2 The individual may have some respiratory problems.
- T1-T6 The person may experience a decrease in pulmonary reserves due to inability to use the intercostal or abdominal muscles.
- T1-T7 The individual may have total capability in the arms but none in the legs. The chest muscles may also be affected.
- T1-T8 The individual may have control of the upper back muscles. The muscles of the abdomen, lower back, and legs will be affected.
- T8 Spinal cord injury above this level may result in an inability to regulate body temperature.
- T12 Spinal cord injury above this level may cause an impaired cough reflex. A person who is unable to generate a forceful cough may have difficulty in clearing a regulator or snorkel.

Lumbar L1-L5

• The individual will have control of the hip joint and may walk fairly well.
• Individuals with lesions above L1 may experience muscle spasms below the level of injury.

Sacral Level

• Control of bowel and bladder function may be affected.

MEDICAL CONCERNS FOR TRAINING AND DIVING

Overview

A number of medical concerns associated with spinal cord injury and scuba diving have been identified. Unfortunately as in many areas of diving, little or no scientific evidence is available to support these concerns. However, as an instructor you should convey this information to your students and assist them in making informed decisions regarding their scuba practices.

Decompression Sickness (DCS)

Many experts have expressed concern regarding a theoretical predisposition to DCS for divers with spinal cord injury. This may be particularly true of divers who continue to dive after spinal cord injury caused by DCS. This theoretical predisposition to DCS is attributed to impaired circulation due to the injury. Another concern is that many of the symptoms associated with DCS are always present in some individuals with spinal cord injury, increasing the difficulty of diagnosing true cases of DCS. However, other experts question the validity of the medical community's assumption that divers with spinal cord injury are more susceptible to DCS.

Implications for Training

The following are suggestions for increasing the safety of divers with spinal cord injury:

- All dives should be considered cold and arduous and bottom times and depths adjusted accordingly.
- The depth and number of repetitive dives should be conservative. Unfortunately, no specific numbers have been established for divers with spinal cord injuries. As with all divers, divers with spinal cord injury must make a personal decision regarding acceptable safety margins.
- The maximum rate of ascent should be 30 feet per minute or less, and safety stops should be performed at the end of every dive. It has also been suggested that divers with spinal cord injury should stop every 15 feet during ascent to allow for adequate outgassing.
- Individuals with a predisposition to DCS may benefit from increased safety margins associated with NITROX or other gas mixtures.

Tissue Breakdown

Due to poor circulation, even minor cuts, scrapes or burns can take a very long time to heal and lead to serious health issues. Furthermore, pressure sores caused by bone pressing against skin for long periods of time can actually lead to a life threatening situation for individuals. These sores can develop into ulcers, known as decubiti, and eat the flesh away to the bone. **Ultimately, such sores can require hospitalization and even prove to be fatal. Treat even minor cuts, scrapes, sores and burns as serious medical concerns.** Frequently, individuals who use wheelchairs will shift in their chairs or actually lift themselves off the seat of the chair. This maneuver, known as depressing, is intended to relieve pressure from sitting too long, and does not mean that they are bored or not paying attention.

Implications for Training

The following are some suggestions for preventing the development of sores, cuts, or scrapes while diving.

- Maintain neutral buoyancy to prevent body parts from dragging on the bottom.
- Divers with asymmetric strength or muscle control may tend to rotate when floating in water, causing body parts to

drag. This rotation can be countered by turning the head. Proper placement of the divers weights can also be effective.

- Use padding such as wet suits, knee pads, shoes or booties, gloves, long sleeve shirts or long pants, to protect any body parts which may drag against hard objects.
- Use padding on the pool deck, the deck of the boat, or any rough or hard surface.
- Use ointments to protect the skin from becoming too soft or dry.
- During the early phases of training, check the skin every 15-20 minutes for any signs of chafing or bruising.
- Be aware that pool lights can generate enough heat to cause serious burns in areas of the body with inadequate circulation. Even lights which are barely warm to the touch can pose a serious hazard to a diver with spinal cord damage.

Bowel and Bladder Control

Spinal cord injury above S2 may result in partial or complete loss of voluntary control of the bowel or bladder. Individuals who do not have control of their bowel or bladder may use a variety of techniques to take care of toilet requirements. One means of bladder management is internal catheterization. This technique involves inserting a catheter into the urethra and draining the urine into a disposable container. Some individuals may choose to use "external plumbing" which consists of an external catheter and tube, and a collection bag worn on the leg. For males the external catheter is similar to a condom except that it has an opening at what is normally the closed end, and is attached to a tube which runs to the collection bag. External plumbing for females consists of an appropriately shaped cup which is sealed with a lubricate and secured by straps. As with the condum type catheter, the cup is attached to a tube which runs to the collection bag. These devices are used by many dry suit divers who do not have spinal cord injury. It is important to make sure that the drainage tube is not twisted or kinked, as that can block the flow of urine, causing a distended bladder. Infections of the urinary tract may be a problem for individuals with spinal cord injury.

Solid waste may be managed through control of the amount of food consumed and regularly scheduled meals. In some cases, the waste must be manually extracted using a "Dill Stick." In other situations, an opening is surgically created in the body and an external collection bag is worn. The surgical procedure used to create the opening is referred to as an ileostomy or colostomy, and the opening itself is referred to as a stoma.

Whether dealing with liquid or solid waste, a strict schedule for diet and personal hygiene can be very important to the health and comfort of the individual. It may be necessary to set aside time in the day's activities to allow for personal hygiene. Also, whether dealing with solid or liquid waste, external collection bags should be emptied prior to any pool sessions. In the case of an individual with a stoma, it may be appropriate to remove the bag and cover the opening with a watertight bandage. This is best determined by consulting both the student and his physician.

Implications for Training

The following are some considerations for managing personal hygiene while scuba diving.

- Divers using collection bags should empty the bag prior to any dive.
- The Handicapped Scuba Association advises that external plumbing can safely be worn under a wet suit as long as care is taken not to pull on, twist or kink the catheter or tubing.
- NOAA suggested that, when possible, the bag remain open throughout the dive and a one way valve be used to prevent water from entering the catheter.
- Some individuals have expressed concern about air being trapped in the tubing or leg bag and reversing the flow of urine.
- Some drugs (alpha blockers) used to aid in bladder control may cause nasal congestion, increasing the possibility of barotrauma.

Autonomic Dysreflexia

Autonomic dysreflexia is a life threatening situation which can occur in individuals with spinal cord damage. This situation is caused by some undesirable stimulus, such as a bent toe, which occurs below the level of the injury. The body senses the problem and attempts to notify the brain.

Unfortunately, because of the neurologic deficit, the message can't get through to the brain. Eventually, in its attempts to warn the brain, the body resorts to raising the blood pressure to dangerous levels. Other signals include slowed heart rate, sweating, pounding headache, goose bumps, vomiting or loss of consciousness. Autonomic dysreflexia is most likely to occur in individuals with injury above T6, but can occur with lesions as low as T10. Be aware that with spinal cord injury above T6 the onset of autonomic dysreflexcia can be sudden. It is a good idea to obtain a statement from the student's physician regarding the frequency and severity of episodes of autonominc dysreflexia. **This can be a life threatening situation and may require immediate medical attention. If there is any question, consult a physician or activate the local Emergency Medical System as necessary.**

Causes of Autonomic Dysreflexia

The following is a list of some of the causes of Autonomic dysreflexia. The list is not meant to be comprehensive, however it does give you an idea of what to consider when diving with people with SCI.

- Full bladder or distended colon (these may be the most common causes)
- Pressure sores
- Cuts or scrapes
- Bent toes or torn or ingrown toenails
- Improperly positioned testicles
- Sunburn

Implications for Training

Autonomic dysreflexia can be caused by any stimulus which would be painful or irritating if spinal cord damage was not

---

present. Unfortunately, a number of causes of autonomic dys-reflexia are present when diving. Divers with spinal cord injury should be advised of these conditions and alerted to take proper precautions.

The following list identifies some of the conditions present in diving which can lead to autonomic dysreflexia. Once again, this list is not comprehensive. It is simply meant to alert you to special concerns for divers with SCI.

- Increased urine output while diving.
- Inadequate toilet facilities at many dive sites or on many dive boats, making it difficult to accommodate toilet requirements.
- "External plumbing" for waste collection, which is twisted, kinked, or blocked due to improper positioning inside the exposure suit.
- Abrasions caused by coral, rocks, or even dive gear such as hard weights or rough straps.
- Sand in the wetsuit causing abrasions.
- Body parts improperly positioned inside of an exposure suit.
- Stings from marine life such as jellyfish or stinging nettles.

First Aid

- Place the individual in a sitting position to lower the blood pressure.
- Loosen any tight clothing or equipment, especially in the abdominal area.
- Ask the person if he or she has attended to their toilet requirements for that day, and check for a full bladder or distended colon.
- Check any "external plumbing" for twists, kinks, or blockages.
- Examine the individual for any potential cause of autonomic dysreflexia such as bent toes, cuts, etc., and correct any problems found.
- Provide basic first aid or life support as necessary.
- When in doubt, call for professional medical help.

Thermoregulation

Individuals with spinal cord injury may have difficulty regulating the temperature in the affected parts of the body. This condition is referred to as Poikilothermy. Depending on the circumstances the individual may experience hypothermia or hyperthermia. Factors affecting the ability to regulate body temperature include:

- the level of the injury
- the amount of muscle atrophy
- spasticity of the muscles
- the percentage of fatty tissue
- the general physical condition of the individual
- the quality of blood circulation in the individual

Implications for Training

It is not uncommon for divers to experience mild hyperthermia or hypothermia. However, for the diver with spinal cord injury this can be a serious situation. Accordingly, you should be aware of the following:

- Monitor students closely for signs of overexposure, especially when in the water or during extreme weather.
- Be prepared to warm up or cool down students showing signs of overexposure. Warm or cool drinks may be called for. It may also be appropriate to have spray bottles available to cool down the student with a spray of water.
- It may be appropriate to have warm packs available to help warm up the student. Do not place the warm pack directly against the student's skin, as it may cause a burn. Instead, wrap it in a towel or similar material and check the skin frequently.
- Fluid intake is important for temperature control. Persons who are active or out in the sun should be advised to drink water every 30 minutes.
- Be cautious about students wearing wet suits in the sun for extended periods of time.
- Be cautious about keeping students in cold water for extended periods of time, especially if they are unable to swim on their own to generate warmth.

- Some students with spinal cord injury may not sweat. Ask them how they feel, and monitor their skin temperature and color.

Individuals with spinal cord injury who experience hypo or hyperthermia may require long periods of time to re-establish an acceptable body temperature. It is best not to let it happen at all. Be conservative with regard to time spent in the water and distance covered during the dive. When diving in cold water, it may be advisable to remain near the exit point and have warming devices prepared.

Spasms

Individuals with injury above L1 may experience muscle spasms below the level of injury. In some cases, spasms can be beneficial, actually assisting in maintaining blood pressure and muscle tone. On the other hand, when they happen at inappropriate times, such as during a transfer from a wheelchair, spasms can be frustrating or even dangerous. In a large person, spasms can occur with such force that you may have difficulty in holding them. Any increase in spasms is a warning of some change taking place with the diver. Spasms can be caused by:

- pressure or touch
- heat
- cold
- stress
- bladder infection
- skin sores or breakdown
- fatigue
- change in position

Implications for Training

- Whether they are intermittent or prolonged, spasms increase the metabolic demand on the diver. This can cause energy reserves to be depleted, leading to early fatigue.

- Spasms interfere with the efficiency of swimming, again leading to early fatigue.
- Spasms may be an indication of the onset of fatigue.
- Spasms may be an indication of the onset of hypothermia.
- Many new divers experience feelings of stress or excitement during the dive. It is important to assist these divers to be calm. Initial dive experiences should be as stress free as possible.
- Some medications used to control spasms may affect the diver's behavior or psychological function. However, when these drugs are used regularly, the effects tend to be minimal. As when any diver uses a drug, you must be concerned with any side effects caused by pressure at depth.

Common Terms

Assistive Devices	Devices which help an individual to perform tasks such as walking, grabbing or holding. Examples of such devices include pointers, special handles, crutches, canes, or walkers.
Involvement	This term refers to any body parts which have been affected by spinal cord injury.
Orthoses	Devices used to correct a deformity, improve function or provide support to prevent collapse. Examples include braces and splints. Orthoses may be referred to by abbreviations such as AFO for ankle-foot orthoses, or HKAFO meaning hip-knee-ankle-foot orthoses.
Paralysis	A condition in which voluntary control of muscle function is lost. However, depending on the nature of the injury, involuntary movements such as muscle spasms may occur. Paralysis may be complete meaning that all voluntary control is lost, or partial/incomplete, meaning some control has been retained.
Paresis	Muscle weakness associated with partial paralysis.

Paraplegia	A condition in which both of the lower limbs are involved to some extent. Trunk balance may also be involved. Many people are surprised to find that some individuals with paraplegia can walk.
Quadriplegia	A condition in which all four of the limbs and the trunk are involved to some extent. Many people are surprised to find that some individuals with quadriplegia can use their arms and/or legs.

CEREBRAL PALSY

Description

Cerebral palsy refers to a group of neurologic disorders which affect both posture and movement. Mild cases of cerebral palsy may result in generalized clumsiness or lack of coordination. Severe cases may result in an inability to perform fine muscle movements or walk or talk. There are a number of classifications for Cerebral palsy, and it is the most commonly found orthopedic disability in the public school systems. This section will discuss the more common effects of Cerebral palsy and some implications for diving.

Spasticity

Approximately 2/3 of the individuals with Cerebral palsy experience muscle spasms and exaggerated reflexes as the primary characteristics of their disorder. This type of Cerebral Palsy is referred to as spasticity, and results in excessive muscle tightness and stiffness. The severity of the spasms will vary from person to person, and for some individuals it may vary from day to day. In some people, the spasms may be mild and intermittent, while for others the spasms may be present all the time. At times, individuals with severe spasticity may need to have their limbs restrained during physical activity.

Individuals with spasticity may experience difficulties with balance, posture or walking, particularly when surfaces are rough or uneven, or when it is necessary to maneuver over or around obstacles. Persons with spasticity may also experience tightness in the arms, causing the arms to be held close to the body with the hands in a fist. Some people experience abnormal reflexes or muscle tightness simply from moving their head. Spasms can be provoked or made worse by cold, fatigue, or some movement patterns.

Athetosis

Athetosis refers to slow, uncontrolled movements. These movements are constant and unpredictable. Approximately 1/4 of those with cerebral palsy have athetosis as the primary characteristic of the disorder.

Constant movement of the head, arms and hands can lead to difficulties in facial expressions, speaking, reading and writing. Individuals with athetosis may also experience problems in activities which require visual focus or tracking objects with their eyes. Many individuals experience difficulty with hand-eye coordination or fine muscle movements.

As with spasticity, the ability to walk may be impaired. Individuals with athetosis who do walk may fall frequently, and they fall backwards more often than they fall forwards.

Implications for Training

- Divers with spasticity should warm-up prior to physical activity.
- Divers with spasticity may have difficulty releasing objects such as the side of the pool, or descent or ascent lines.
- The diver may experience difficulty holding the regulator in his mouth.
- Individuals with spasticity may tend to rotate when floating in the water. This rotation may be countered by turning the head. Proper positioning of the diver's weights can also be effective.

- Divers with cerebral palsy may or may not require assistance when putting on a wetsuit.
- Divers with cerebral palsy may or may not be able to swim and kick effectively with fins.
- Wearing a wet suit may actually help control some involuntary movements.
- Wearing a wet suit may actually inhibit some voluntary movements.

Individuals with cerebral palsy may find being in the water makes it easier to stand up. However, this improved balance may be lost when wearing scuba gear. It may be advisable to

FIGURE 2-1

have flotation devices such as surf mats available even in shallow water, so the students can use them for support while standing. It is also important that students have confidence in flotation provided by wet suits and buoyancy control devices. In the initial phases of training, I tell the student that his buddy or a staff member should always be close enough for him to grab if necessary. However, the buddy or staff member should not grab the student unless it is absolutely necessary. As the training progresses, I encourage the student to rely on the support of the water and his equipment. The amount of support necessary will be determined by the student's abilities and comfort level in the water. In figure 2-1 notice how the diver is using a boogie board for support while standing in the shallow section of the pool. Also notice the knee pads worn by the diver to prevent cuts and scrapes.

Common Terms

Diplegia   This term implies that the lower limbs are much more involved than the upper limbs.

Hemiplegia   This term implies complete involvement of one side of the body or the other.

Triplegia   This term implies that three limbs, typically both legs and one arm, are involved.

AMPUTATION

Amputations or missing limbs can occur as a result of illness, injury or birth defect. When a person is born missing a limb, this is known as a congenital amputation. A person with a congenital amputation may be missing the entire limb. However, in some cases the middle portion of the limb is missing, resulting in a foot attached directly to the hip, or a hand directly to the shoulder. The extent of the disability will be determined by the number of limbs amputated and how much of the limb remains.

Implications for Training

• It may be necessary to pad the stump of a surgically amputated limb.

- Divers with amputations may have unusual buoyancy characteristics. Typically they will roll towards the side of the body where the limbs are still present. For example, a diver missing his right arm will typically roll to the left. Creative weight placement may be called for to achieve proper buoyancy and trim.
- Many individuals with amputations prefer to swim on their back.

Individuals who have had surgical amputation may have a predisposition to DCS. The issue here is not the missing limb but the scar tissue which may result from the surgery itself. The site of any injury is considered a possible predisposing factor to DCS for any diver, and a surgical amputation is not an exception. The amount of scar tissue present will vary based on the site and reason for the amputation, so it is advisable to consult the diver's physician. Regardless, just like divers with spinal cord injury, divers with surgical amputations must establish their own personal safety margins for time and depth as well as ascent rate and safety stops.

Common Terms

An amputation may be referred to by the site of the amputation, and frequently abbreviations are used. For instance, AK refers to an amputation through or above the knee joint, while BE refers to an amputation below the elbow, but above or through the wrist. You will also see terminology such as single or double, indicating the number of limbs amputated. Double BK indicates a double below-the-knee amputation. You may also see amputations described as combined, indicating a combination of upper and lower limb amputations.

Phantom Limb	A phenomenon in which some individuals with amputations experience sensations such as itching or pain as if the limb is still present.
Prostheses	Refers to a device used to replace or substitute for a missing limb.
Stump	The end of a limb which has been amputated.

GENERAL HEALTH CONCERNS

Overview

Some individuals with disabilities may have health issues which are not caused directly by the disability. For instance, some people with disabilities lead sedentary lifestyles even though they are capable of getting out and being active. This sedentary lifestyle is not necessarily caused by the disability itself, but may result from fear of reinjury or social embarrassment. Nevertheless, this lifestyle can result in issues which have implications for scuba diving. This section will discuss some of these issues such as obesity, low levels of physical fitness, osteoporosis, and soft tissue injuries. A few other concerns which are not health related but which may be more extreme among divers with disabilities will also be discussed. Implications for scuba training will also be presented.

Obesity and Low Levels of Physical Fitness

A sedentary lifestyle can lead to low levels of physical fitness or obesity. There may also be concerns regarding cardiovascular health. These individuals may find it extremely difficult to meet the normal physical demands of scuba diving, much less the demands which can occur in an emergency. It is also important to keep in mind that compared to a student without a disability, a student with a disability may often expend more energy to accomplish the same task. For example, a diver who uses fins gets most of his propulsion from the large leg muscles. However, a diver who doesn't use fins must rely on the muscles of the upper body, and this can be very demanding. Once again, it is important not to generalize and to consider the individual diver in question. The ability to meet the physical demands of diving will vary from individual to individual, and a physically fit diver with a disability may be better prepared to meet these challenges than a diver without a disability but who is not physically fit.

Prior to accepting any student into training, it is wise to discuss the planned activities with the student and possibly his physician. Any student whose level of fitness is inadequate

---

Medical Aspects

for scuba training should be encouraged to initiate an appropriate program of exercise. With those students who are accepted into the program, be careful that they don't overdo it. It is natural to want to keep up with the group, and in the case of a student with a disability, the student may feel that he has something to prove. On the other hand, some experienced adapted scuba instructors feel that students with disabilities have a better awareness of their bodies and abilities than students without disabilities. As always, it is best to be open and honest with your students and to encourage them to take the same approach with you.

Implications for Training

- Evaluate the physical fitness and abilities of all students on an individual basis.
- Plan dive activities, such as surface swims, which are within the abilities of the students. It is good to challenge them and help them establish their physical limits. However, be careful not to set them up to fail.
- Encourage students to participate in appropriate exercise programs.

Osteoporosis

Loss of calcium in bone tissue may also be a concern for individuals who lead a sedentary lifestyle. This process, known as osteoporosis, causes the bones to become brittle and more susceptible to fracture. The course of osteoporosis may also affect an individual's strength.

Implications for training

- Be cautious whenever you are in physical contact, such as assisting with a transfer.
- Warn the diver to exercise care when handling heavy or hard objects such as tanks and weight belts.
- In some cases it may be safest to have the student handle the gear only when they are in the water and not on dry land. This way they can take advantage of the buoyancy of the water and minimize the risk of injury.

Soft Tissue Injuries

People who use wheelchairs or other assistive devices may be prone to soft tissue injuries, especially in the arms and shoulders. This may be an issue when handling hard, heavy objects such as tanks and weight belts. It may also be an issue for a diver who is an upper body swimmer. Unlike lap swimming, scuba requires that the diver move through the water while wearing bulky scuba gear.

Implications for Training

* Emphasize the importance of neutral buoyancy to minimize stress and strain.
* Emphasize the importance of streamlining to minimize drag.
* Warn the student to exercise care when handling equipment which is heavy or hard.

Other Issues

Some instructors experienced with teaching individuals with disabilities have identified other issues as being more common among these divers. Some of these issues include anxiety, fear of falling, fear of mishandling, and problems with balance or vertigo.

Implications for Training

* Identify any problems or issues of concern.
* It may be helpful to explain that many students, both with and without disabilities, experience the same concerns.
* It may also be helpful to have the student talk with a diver who has had similar experiences.
* Ideally, these issues should be resolved without making a big deal of them.

GENERAL CONSIDERATIONS FOR TRAVEL

Overview

Any special concerns or needs of individuals with disabilities may become more difficult to address when traveling. Obviously, this will be determined by the severity of any disability and the creativity of those involved. The following are some of the issues to consider when planning a dive trip. The information presented focuses on airplanes because they are frequently involved in dive travel. However, many of the same issues apply to trains, buses or boats.

A list of travel resources for individuals with disabilities is provided at the end of this section.

- Many facilities or boats advertised as accessible are not truly easily accessed by a person who uses a wheelchair. It may be best to have the traveler with the disability talk to the people at the facility prior to the trip. This will allow the traveler to develop realistic expectations. It will also allow the facility to prepare.
- It has been my experience that wherever you go, people are willing to help. However, you must be prepared to give them guidance, be patient, and work together.
- When staying in unfamiliar hotels or resorts, find out in advance the status of restroom facilities, showers, eating areas, boats, boat docks and beaches. Be aware that many ramps are short and steep, making it difficult for some individuals to push their chairs up unassisted.
- Airports and airplanes can pose logistical challenges. Some airlines may have room for an individual to bring a wheelchair on the plane. Other airlines may require that wheelchairs be checked as baggage. In this case, it will be necessary to arrange for transfers on and off the plane at all points in the trip. Make sure to make these arrangements when you book the flight, and confirm them at every stage of the trip. Also keep in mind that wheel-

chairs are personal and expensive. Do everything possible to make sure that the chair makes the same trip as everyone else.

- Some airplanes may have "aisle chairs" on board during the flight. These are narrow wheelchairs that fit in the aisle of the plane. These chairs can be used to transfer on and off the plane, as well as to move about during the flight. However, not all planes have these chairs onboard, so if someone needs to move during the flight, it may be necessary to carry or otherwise assist them.

- It is always possible that the plane will be delayed in the air or on the ground, so it may be wise to carry extra containers for waste collection. Blankets can be used for privacy.

- Long airplane flights can contribute to dehydration as the air is dehumidified. Travelers should be cautioned to drink plenty of water.

- Changes in diet and eating schedules may require adjustment for travelers with disabilities. Be aware that personal hygiene programs might be disrupted.

- When staying in hotels, be aware of emergency exit procedures. In the event that elevators are not an option, some individuals may find it difficult or impossible to use stairs. It may be appropriate to request rooms on the ground floor.

- The needs of a diver with a severe disability can increase the work load of staff or crew significantly. When putting together a group of divers to travel, make sure the facility and staff are adequate to meet the needs of all the divers. Factors such as boat design, experience of the divers, boat crew or resort staff, and the willingness of the group to work together, are all important factors in determining an appropriate number of divers.

CHAPTER SUMMARY

Divers with disabilities may have physical or medical issues which must be addressed to ensure their safety and comfort. Some of these issues may stem directly from the disability, while others may or may not be related. Regardless, it is important that you, the instructor, familiarize yourself with any special needs your student might have. You must also familiarize yourself with any special risks associated with that student's medical history. This means that while you educate the student and perhaps his physician about scuba, you must also educate yourself about the disability in question. In many cases the individual with the disability may be the best resource available for information regarding the disability. It is in his best interest to know as much as possible about the disability. Keep in mind however that the student's desire to scuba dive may cause him to have an overly optimistic perspective regarding his needs and abilities. Information about various disabilities can also be found at the library, through local medical schools, the student's physician or the Divers Alert Network.

Understanding the needs of your students will also enhance the enjoyment and success of everybody involved. Furthermore, it will assist you in screening students, setting schedules, and planning activities which have the greatest likelihood of success. It will also help ease the way when you go on dive trips.

Remember that it is not necessary to become a walking medical encyclopedia. What is necessary is a willingness to do a little homework. Combined with honest and open communication among you, your student, and the physician, this should be all that is necessary for a safe and successful scuba experience.

REVIEW OF MAIN POINTS

- When screening any student consider the abilities of the student, as well as his or her mental, emotional and medical fitness.
- When evaluating a student's water abilities, focus on safe, effective technique rather than style.
- If a student has a severe disability, evaluate his or her ability to roll over from front to back, and ability to stand up unassisted in shallow water.
- A person with a disability may be very physically fit.
- Spinal cord injury refers to a neurologic deficit of the spine.

- Typically, the higher the level of injury to the spine, the more severe the disability.
- The degree to which voluntary control and sensation are lost is determined by the severity of the injury to the spinal cord.
- The effects of two spinal cord injuries which occur at the same level may not be the same.
- Individuals with paraplegia may be able to use their legs.
- Individuals with quadriplegia may be able to use their arms and/or legs.
- Divers with disabilities may be more susceptible to DCS.
- Divers with disabilities may be more susceptible to tissue breakdown. Untreated sores can be fatal for divers with disabilities.
- **Treat even minor cuts, scrapes, sores and burns as serious medical concerns.**
- Diet and a regular meal schedule may be important factors in personal hygiene for divers with disabilities.
- **Autonomic dysreflexia can be a life threatening situation for divers with spinal cord injury and can be provoked by a number of stimuli present in scuba diving.**
- **Divers with spinal cord injury may be more susceptible to hypo- or hyperthermia.**
- Involuntary muscle spasms can interfere with swimming and increase the demand for energy expenditure, causing fatigue.
- Cerebral palsy is a disorder which affects both posture and movement.
- Divers with spastic cerebral palsy should warm up prior to any activity.
- Divers with athetosis may exhibit constant movements which are involuntary and unpredictable.
- Divers with amputations may be more susceptible to DCS.
- Divers with amputations will typically have unusual buoyancy characteristics.
- Individuals with disabilities may be more prone to obesity, low physical fitness or osteoporosis resulting from a sedentary lifestyle.

- Individuals who use assistive devices such as wheelchairs may experience a high rate of soft tissue injuries.
- Anxiety, fear of falling or being mishandled, vertigo, and problems with balance may be more extreme among divers with disabilities.
- Common inconveniences associated with travel may be more significant for travelers with disabilities. It is important to plan ahead to make sure that any special needs will be taken care of.

APPLYING YOUR KNOWLEDGE

1. Discuss medical and physical ability criteria which should be considered when evaluating a prospective candidate for scuba training.
2. Identify the various regions of the spine and describe common effects of injury at the various regions.
3. Compare and contrast complete versus incomplete spinal cord injury.
4. Identify common medical concerns associated with scuba training for individuals with spinal cord injury, and describe implications for training these individuals.
5. Identify terms commonly associated with Spinal Cord Injury and provide a definition for each.
6. Describe two types Cerebral Palsy and identify implications for scuba training for individuals with Cerebral Palsy.
7. Identify terms commonly associated with Cerebral Palsy and provide a definition for each.
8. Identify the various causes of amputation.
9. Discuss the medical concerns and implications for scuba training for individuals with amputation.
10. Identify terms commonly associated with amputation and provide a definition for each.
11. Discuss some general health concerns for individuals with disabilities and explain training implications for each.
12. Identify issues which may arise for an individual with a disability while traveling and explain how these issues may be addressed.

REFERENCES

Council for National Cooperation in Aquatics (1982). Aquatics now. In R. D. Clayton (Ed.), Holiday Inn and the Ohio State University Columbus Ohio Council for National Cooperation in Aquatics (pp. 179-187). Indianapolis,IN: Author.

Emmerson, L., Ravendale, J., Atterbury, S., Isabelle, H., North York Y-Nauts, Toronto Snorkelauts, Carmichael, B., Garrett, G., & Murray, R. (n.d.). Skin diving for the physically handicapped. (Available from Moray Wheels Adaptive Scuba Association, PO Box 1660 GMF, Boston, MA. 02205).

Handicapped Scuba Association. (1987). H.S.A. instructor's manual. Available from Handicapped Scuba Association 1104 El Prado, San (Clemente, CA. 92672).

Jankowski, L. W. (1995). Teaching persons with disabilities to scuba diving. (Available from Quebec Underwater Federation / F.Q.A.S. (Fédération Québécoise des Activitiés Subaquatiques) 4545, ave Pierre-De Coubertin, C.P. 1000, succ. M Montréal (Québec) CANADA H1V 3R2.

Lin, L. Y.(1987). Scuba divers with disabilities challenge medical protocols and ethics. The Physician and Sports Medicine, 15 (6), 224-235.

National Association of Underwater Instructors (1995). NAUI professional liability insurance and risk management recommendations [Brochure]. Montclair, CA: Author.

National Oceanic and Atmospheric Administration (1991). Diving with disabilities. In NOAA diving manual diving for science and technology (pp. A1-A11). Silver Spring, MD: National Oceanic and Atmospheric Administration.

Petrofsky, J. S. (1994). Diving with spinal cord injury. Palaestra, 11(1), 30-31, 49-51.

Sherrill C. (1993). Adapted physical activity, recreation and sport: Crossdisciplinary and lifespan (4th ed.). WCB Brown & Benchmark: Dubuque.

Waring, W. (1984). Concerns for diving in the spinal cord injury population. Paper presented at the national conference of the Council for National Cooperation in Aquatics, Fort Worth , TX.

Water Sports Division of the British Sports Association for the Disabled. (1983). Water sports for the disabled (pp. 112-126). West Yorkshire: EP Publishing Ltd..

Williamson, J. A., McDonald, R. W., Galligan, E. A., Baker, P.G., & Hammond, C. T. D. (1984). Selection and training of disabled persons for scuba diving Medical and psychological aspects. The medical journal of australia, 141, 414-418.

RESOURCES FOR TRAVELERS
WITH DISABILITIES

Accessible Journeys 35 W. Sellers Ave., Ridley Park, PA 19078	800-846-4537 610-521-0339
Directions Unlimited 720 N. Bedford Rd., Bedford Hills, NY 10507	914-241-1700
Flying Wheels Travel 143 W. Bridge St., Owatonna, MN 55060	800-535-6790 In MN 507-451-5005
Imperial Travel 717 17th St. Lobby Level, Denver CO 80202	303-292-1334
Mobility International USA Box 3551, Eugene, OR 97403	503-343-1284
New Directions 5276 Hollister Ave., No. 207, Santa Barbara, CA 93111	805-967-2841
Society for the Advancement of Travel for the Handicapped (SATH) 347 5th Ave. Suite 610, New York, NY 10016	212-447-0027
Wilderness Inquiry 1313 Fifth St. SE, Box 84, Minneapolis, MN 55414-1546	800-728-0719 612-379-3858

The information above was taken from an article entitled *"IS THE TRAVEL INDUSTRY COMPLYING WITH THE LAW?"*. The article was authored by Emma Edmunds and was published in the January 1993 issue of <u>Travel & Leisure</u> magazine.

Chapter 3

Equipment

CHAPTER OVERVIEW

Scuba diving is an equipment intensive sport, and selecting the appropriate equipment is important for any diver. When choosing their equipment, most divers consider fit, function, and cost, although not necessarily in that order. In recent times, given the wide range of styles in equipment, many divers also consider color, style, and appearance to be important. For a diver with a disability, these factors may assume even greater importance.

This section will present information regarding general considerations for selection, configuration, and use of standard items of equipment. Suggestions will also be offered regarding specific items of equipment such as regulators, snorkels, exposure suits, etc.

GENERAL CONSIDERATIONS

Many experts have identified proper equipment as essential to the safety, comfort, and enjoyment of divers with disabilities. Some experienced instructors feel that no equipment modifications are necessary, while others feel that special designs or modifications can contribute significantly to the ease, safety and enjoyment of the dive. As with any diver, equipment realities for divers with disabilities vary with the diver. Some may modify the gear out of need, while others may do so out of the desire to tinker or improve. Still others may choose not to modify their gear even if it might make things easier.

IMPLICATIONS FOR SELECTION AND USE OF EQUIPMENT

- Never modify gear in a manner which makes it unsafe.
- Modifying equipment may void any manufacturer's warranty.
- A diver with disability may want her gear to look as conventional as possible to avoid calling attention to her disability.
- It may be advantageous to set up or wear the gear in an unconventional manner. For example, it may be advantageous to configure the gear to take advantage of greater strength, dexterity or range of motion on one side of the body. Snorkels, gauges, or even primary regulators may be worn on either the left or right side of the body.
- Light weight, high performance equipment may be preferable for divers with limited physical abilities.
- For a diver with limited strength, mobility, or ability to shout, an audio or visual signaling device may be of extra benefit and importance. Ideally, the diver should be able to use this device without assistance.

REGULATORS

Some divers may lack strength or control of the facial muscles, making it difficult to retain the regulator in the mouth. Other divers may be unable to exhale forcefully, making it difficult to clear a regulator.

Implications for Selection and Use

- Lightweight regulators require less strength to hold in the mouth.
- Low volume regulators are typically easier to clear.
- Purge buttons should be easy to manipulate.
- High performance regulators typically require less effort to breathe.
- Custom or specialized mouthpieces may make it easier to retain the regulator.
- A strap can help hold the regulator in or near the mouth, making it easier to retrieve the regulator.

- For some divers, it may be advisable to use a full face mask, or mouthpiece such as in communication systems.
- Remember that anything which makes it difficult to remove the regulator from the mouth will also make it difficult for the diver to share air from another diver's tank.

Inability to retrieve the extra second stage may be an issue. For a diver with limited dexterity, it may be advisable to strap the octopus to her forearm. Low profile second stages on a long hose work well for this application. Position the regulator on the diver's strong side and fasten it so that it can't slip or rotate. Velcro straps work well as fasteners, but be prepared to use two or three.

SNORKELS

Some divers may lack strength or control of the facial muscles, making it difficult to retain the snorkel in the mouth. Other divers may be unable to exhale forcefully, making it difficult to clear the snorkel.

Implications for Selection and Use

- Self-draining or purge snorkels are easier to clear.
- Snorkels with splash guards are easier to clear and require clearing less often.
- Custom or orthodontic mouthpieces make it easier to retain the snorkel.
- If a student is unable to clear the snorkel effectively, or is likely to lose the snorkel and would have difficulty retrieving it, you must be extremely cautious. It may be necessary to provide the student with a readily accessible back-up air supply. **It is important to know whether or not the diver can roll over unassisted from front to back, and to monitor that diver closely at all times.**

MASKS

Students who lack control of their facial muscles may have difficulty finding a mask that fits. Also, a diver who does not use fins but swims with his upper body, may find it inconvenient to use his hands when clearing their mask.

Implications for Selection and Use

- For some students it may be advisable to use a full face mask. Be aware that this can complicate air sharing techniques.
- Masks with purge valves do not require use of the hands when clearing water from the mask. However, some masks have a bulky purge valve, making it difficult to access the nose for ear clearing. This may be particularly true for divers with limited manual dexterity.
- Wide soft straps may be easier to manipulate than the traditional split mask strap.

BUOYANCY COMPENSATORS

Some divers will have limited dexterity, range of motion and strength. Other divers may have atrophied lower limbs. As much as possible, the buoyancy compensator (BC) selected should accommodate the diver's needs. Also, some divers may require assistance when putting on the BC. These divers should select a BC which is easy to manipulate by either the diver or the buddy. Also keep in mind that some divers lack the use of the abdominal and leg muscles or have a weak lower body. For these divers, balance can be an issue, making selection of the proper BC important for both safety and comfort. Be prepared to experiment with styles and sizing.

Implications for Selection and Use

- Controls on the BC should be as large and prominent as possible. Buttons should stick up as opposed to being recessed. One example of increasing the size of controls is to attach a regulator stress reliever or large ball to the end of the dump valve cord.
- Ideally, the controls should not require a great deal of strength to operate.
- As much as possible get the controls on the strong side of the diver. For example, it is not typically possible to put the inflation mechanism on the right side of the BC. However, some BCs have dump valves or overpressure valves on the right side. For divers with limited ability on the left side of the body it may be possible to rig the right side of the BC to allow for easier deflation techniques.

- Inflation assemblies which include low pressure air infla
tion from the regulator ("power inflators") and can also
activate the rapid exhaust valve allow complete buoyancy
control with one hand. For divers who may have limited
range of motion, the length of the corrugated hose con-
necting the inflator assembly and the BC itself can be cus-
tomized so the inflator will hang at just the right spot.
- BC's with front adjustable straps and quick release buckles make it much easier for divers with limited range of
motion to put on or take off the BC. They also make it easier for the buddy to help.

Weight Integrated Buoyancy Compensators

The following information applies to BCs designed by the
manufacturer to integrate the weight system. Be aware that
putting weights in the pocket of a BC which is not designed
to integrate the weights can compromise the ability to quickly dump the weights in an emergency.

Advantages

- The need for putting on a separate weight system, which can
require strength and dexterity, is eliminated. Even if the
buddy would normally put the belt on the diver, integrated
systems eliminate one step in the preparation process.
- The need for tightening the weight belt to compensate for
wetsuit compression at depth is eliminated.
- The problem of weight belts pressing on the stomach or
diaphragm and inhibiting breathing is eliminated.
- Concerns about hard bulky weights pressing against the
diver's body and causing cuts or bruises are eliminated.
- The risk of accidentally losing the weight system is
reduced. This may be particularly true of divers with atrophied lower limbs who may find it difficult to keep a traditional weight belt from slipping down or even off.

Disadvantages

- Integrated systems combine the weight of the belt and the
tank, making the system much heavier than the conventional scuba set up.

- On the surface integrated systems may have a tendency to push the diver onto his stomach. This is determined, at least to some extent by the amount of air in the BC, the amount and position of the weight worn, and the design of the BC itself. In some cases, this tendency to push forward can actually be an asset. I find it particularly useful when the diver is at depth and wants to assume a standing position. The forward push of the BC can counteract the tendency of the tank to pull the diver onto his back, and the diver can be supported in an upright position.
- If the weights are dumped, retrieving them and replacing them in the BC is more cumbersome than retrieving a weight belt. However, the risk of this happening is low.

Full Front Inflation Buoyancy Compensators

Some instructors prefer full front inflation BCs for training. Some divers find this style of BC provides better buoyancy control and reduces the risk of a face-down situation when the BC is inflated at the surface. The cylinder can be adjusted up or down to avoid pulling the diver onto his back.

WEIGHT SYSTEMS

Many divers may experience difficulty with conventional weight belts. These difficulties may stem from lack of strength, dexterity or range of motion. Common problems include:

- Difficulty with weight belts slipping or rotating due to atrophied lower limbs.
- Weight belts pressing on the stomach and interfering with breathing.
- Hard bulky weights causing bruising.
- Weight belts interfering with mobility of the hip for walking or kicking.
- Buckles being difficult to manipulate.

Implications for Training
- Soft pouch weights are less likely to cause bruises or cuts.

- Suspender weight systems may be appropriate for divers with atrophied lower limbs, or impaired strength, dexterity, range of motion, or respiration.
- BCs designed by the manufacturer to integrate the weights may be appropriate for divers with atrophied lower limbs, or impaired strength, dexterity, range of motion, or respiration.
- Weight belts which automatically compensate for wetsuit compression may be appropriate for divers who find it difficult to manipulate buckles.
- The buoyancy characteristics of the diver may make it necessary to place weights in different locations such as around the ankles, upper legs, forearms, or tank valve. These weights may be traditional ankle weights fastened with quick release buckles or Velcro. They may also be contained in pouches, or fastened with snap hooks, or Velcro straps. Pockets can be sewn onto the exposure suit itself.
- Regardless of the location of the weight or method of attachment, the diver or buddy must always be able to dump enough weight with a "quick release" to ensure positive buoyancy of the diver. **Never compromise the safety of the diver with unsafe weighting techniques.**

FINS

Some divers with disabilities may use fins while others will not.

Implications for Training

- Fins may add stability for divers who are unable to kick. However, they may also make the diver more cumbersome. It is worth experimenting to find out.
- Divers who can use fins effectively when wearing just a bathing suit or thin warm water wetsuit may not be able to kick against the resistance of a cold water wetsuit.
- Some divers who are upper body swimmers may increase their propulsion by using webbed gloves, hand paddles or other specially designed devices to. Other divers may feel that such devices are cumbersome and cause them to lose dexterity.

- Divers with a below-the-knee (BK) amputation may be able to place the fin directly on the stump. The fin could be attached by running straps from both sides of the fin to a belt located somewhere above the point of amputation.
- Other divers with amputations of the lower limbs may attach a fin to a prosthetic device.

In their book *Diving with Disabilities*, Jill Robinson and Dale Fox offer the following suggestions for divers who use prosthetic devices:

- Avoid using materials which will corrode in salt water.
- Consider the buoyancy characteristics of the prostheses. If it is either too positive or too negative, it will affect the diver's trim.
- Use of a wooden leg allows for a variety of methods for attaching the fin, including Velcro, screws, glue or some combination of fasteners.
- Prostheses can be designed which allow the foot position to be adjusted to accommodate either walking or kicking with fins.

EXPOSURE SUITS

Most divers today wear some type of exposure suits in all but the warmest water. Exposure suits may be of special importance to divers who have difficulty regulating their body temperature. Unfortunately, many divers may have difficulty putting on their wetsuits either alone or unassisted.

Implications for Training

- When assisting a diver putting on a suit, be careful not to knock the diver off balance.
- When assisting a diver sitting in a wheel chair to put on a suit, be sure that the chair is secured and the brakes are on. If the diver is in a power chair, be sure that it is turned off.
- Wet suits can be modified to incorporate long zippers and gussets to make them easier to get on or off. Unfortunately, even when a dam is provided to block water penetration, many divers feel that suits with zippers are not as warm as

suits with fewer and smaller zippers. This is more of an issue in colder water.

- Divers can lubricate themselves or the suit with powder, soapy water, shampoo or other mild lubricants. Check with the suit manufacturer to ensure that you won't damage the suit. Also be aware of the possible impact of the lubricant on the diver's skin and the environment.
- Today, many undergarments are available which are designed to be worn under the wet suit. These garmets make it easier both to put on and remove the wet suit, as well as providing some extra warmth.
- When assisting a diver to put on a suit, be careful not to pull on or kink any external plumbing.
- When assisting a diver to put on a suit, be careful with body parts such as fingers, fingernails, toes, toenails, or testicles.
- When assisting the diver to put on wet suit bottoms, it may be appropriate for the assistant to slide her hand up through the pant leg. Place your hand through the opening for the ankle and foot and reach up towards the crotch area. This will allow you to cover the foot and toes, as shown in

FIGURE 3-1

figure 3-1, preventing toes from being bent or toenails being torn. As you guide the foot and leg through the pant leg, be careful not to pull too hard. A similar technique can also be used for guiding the hand and arm through the jacket sleeve.

- For divers with limited range of motion or strength on one side of the body, it may be best always to start on a particular side of the body.
- Divers with loss of sensation who use dry suits should be very aware of suit squeeze. Because these divers can't feel the squeeze, they can actually be bruised without knowing it. Appropriate training is important for any diver who uses a dry suit.
- Some divers may find boots with zippers easier to get on and off. Boots may be lubricated or slippery socks may be worn. Take care to check that the toes are properly positioned in the boot.
- Some divers may prefer gloves with zippers or a three finger mitten as opposed to a five finger glove. Gloves can be lubricated, and it is important to check that the fingers are properly positioned.

CYLINDERS

For some divers, the major concerns about tanks are the ease with which the valve can be manipulated, and the tank's effect on the divers balance, trim or buoyancy. The weight of the tank may be an issue for divers who lack strength, while other divers may be more concerned with the quantity of air the tank will provide. As always, these are personal decisions which must be made by the diver.

Implications for Training

- As the size and strength of the diver varies, so will the affect of the tank on buoyancy, balance and trim. Experiment with different tanks to see what works best.
- Tanks which are long enough to rest on the bottom, floor, or pool or boat deck may eliminate the need for the student to support the weight of the tank while performing skills, putting on or taking off gear, or waiting for a

buddy. This may be helpful to students who lack strength, stamina or balance.

- Divers with limited dexterity or hand strength may require valves with large on/off knobs which are easy to turn.
- When considering the size of the air supply, keep in mind that for any diver, air consumption will vary based on the activity level of the dive and the skills and fitness level of the diver. Also, keep in mind that divers with disabilities frequently must expend more energy to accomplish the same amount of physical work as a diver without a disability.
- The size of the air supply needed may be determined by the length of time the diver can spend in the water without becoming cold or tired.

HAND HELD EQUIPMENT

Many pieces of equipment typically occupy the diver's hands or arms when being used. Examples of such equipment include compasses, lights, reels, or the diver's console. For divers who use fins, these objects can be used while swimming. However, for a diver who swims with his upper body, use of these objects may interrupt his swimming. In the case of a diver who must expend considerable effort to swim or at least to get started swimming, this can be inconvenient.

Implications for Training

- A number of products are available on the market today which allow lights to be attached to the head, the mask strap, or to other equipment.
- Keep in mind that for night diving the diver must be able to give signals with his light.
- A number of devices are available which allow the console to be worn so as to be visible without having to use the hands.
- The diver should be trained in natural navigation to minimize the need to check his compass.
- Divers and instructors may need to be creative to satisfy specific needs or desires.

CHAPTER SUMMARY

Scuba diving is an equipment intensive sport, making it important that all divers select equipment appropriate for their abilities and their dive activities. Criteria to consider when selecting equipment include fit, function, and cost. Many scuba divers with special needs use conventional equipment, helping to hold down the expense of the sport. Unfortunately, in some cases using conventional equipment may cause the diver to sacrifice safety, convenience or comfort. Some divers modify standard equipment or manufacture custom gear to satisfy their needs. These divers avoid sacrificing convenience or comfort but probably spend more money to do so. Depending on how the equipment is modified, the diver may or may not compromise safety. Ultimately, the objective is to use equipment which will safely accommodate the diver's abilities. Equipment which is properly designed, properly configured and properly used will maximize the safety, comfort and enjoyment of the diver.

REVIEW OF MAIN POINTS

- Never modify or configure gear in an unsafe manner.
- Configure gear so as to take advantage of the diver's strengths and abilities.
- Light weight, high performance regulators may be preferable for divers with limited physical abilities.
- Regulators should offer ease of breathing and clearing.
- Some divers may have difficulty retrieving the extra second stage. It may be advisable to strap the octopus to the diver's arm.
- Self draining snorkels with splash guards may be necessary for divers with impaired respiration or ability to cough.
- Masks with purge valves leave the hands free when clearing the mask. However the purge valve may block access to the nose for ear clearing.
- BC controls should be as large and prominent as possible. They should also require minimal strength to operate.
- Front adjustable straps and quick release buckles make the BC easy to put on or take off.

- Weight integrated BC systems offer many advantages to divers with special needs. However, depending on the design and usage, the BC can push the diver face down in the water.
- Divers with limited dexterity may find it preferable to use a weight system which automatically compensates for wetsuit compression.
- Weight belts may interfere with breathing, kicking or walking for some divers.
- Some divers with leg amputations may be able to attach a fin directly to the stump. Divers who use prosthetic devices may design custom prostheses to accommodate their fins.
- Wetsuits can be extremely difficult for divers with disabilities to put on, requiring tremendous energy expenditure. The suits can be lubricated or modified with long zippers and gussets to make them easier to put on.
- When assisting a diver to put on the wetsuit, be careful not to pull on, twist or kink any "external plumbing". Also take care not to pull on or injure body parts such fingers, toes, testicles, etc.
- Boots and gloves with zippers may be easier for the diver to put on.
- Tank valves with large on/off knobs may be easier for the diver to manipulate.
- The size, weight, and position of the tank can have tremendous impact on the divers buoyancy, balance and trim.
- A diver who swims with her upper body may want to minimize the amount of gear or tasks which require the use of hor hands.

APPLYING YOUR KNOWLEDGE

1. Discuss general implications for selection and use of equipment for divers with special needs.
2. Discuss implications for selection and use of the following pieces of equipment: regulators, snorkels, masks, weight systems, fins, exposure suits, tanks, and hand-held equipment.

3. Discuss factors to be considered when selecting a BC for a diver with special needs.

4. Describe the advantages and disadvantages of weight integrated buoyancy systems.

REFERENCES

Brabant, J. (1983). Scuba diving for the disabled. Sports 'N Spokes, 9, 9-11.

Buckley, J. (1994, June 27). Set free undersea. Sports Illustrated, 80 (25).

Carroll, J. F. (1987). Scuba diving with disabilities. Sports 'N Spokes, 13, 45-47.

Garrett, G. (1983). An analysis of a therapeutic rehabilitative activity: Scuba diving. Unpublished master's thesis, Tufts University.

National Oceanic and Atmospheric Administration (1991). Diving with disabilities. In NOAA diving manual diving for science and technology (pp. A1-A11). Silver Spring, MD: National Oceanic and Atmospheric Administration.

Open Waters (1994). Open waters scuba diving for everyone: A guide to making diving training accessible to people with disabilities. (Available from Open Waters c/o Alpha One, 127 Main St., South Portland, ME 04106)

Petrofsky, J. S. (1994). Diving with spinal cord injury. Palaestra, 11(1), 30-31, 49-51.

Chapter 4

Teaching Techniques

CHAPTER OVERVIEW

Just as you will see differences in all of your students, you will also see differences in the ways they perform the various scuba skills. As an instructor it is important that you distinguish between techniques that are unsafe and those that are simply different. When I began working with students with special needs, I was forced to analyze not only the skills I taught, but the way I taught them. In doing so, I realized that for some skills, steps that I had considered fundamental to proper performance were not really a safety issue. Instead, these steps had been included to increase the comfort and convenience of the student diver. Unfortunately for some students, these "steps of convenience" actually increase the difficulty of the skill. As instructors, it is important that we allow each student to develop her own style as long as it does not compromise her safety. As I heard a divemaster say, "It doesn't matter if they get it done ugly, as long as they get it done." Personally, I like to substitute the word "differently" for the word "ugly," but the point is that we should be concerned about safety over style.

When working with students with special needs, you will find that many of the techniques you already teach will work just fine with little or no modification. In other cases you may have to make major modifications or start from scratch. Patience, creativity and objectivity will help a great deal in developing techniques which are safe and effective for your students. Ultimately, you will probably find that the techniques developed by and for students with special needs will also make life easier for all of your students.

This chapter will present suggestions for teaching and performing basic scuba skills. To avoid repetition, equipment will not be discussed in great detail, as it has already been discussed in another section. However, where it seems appropriate, information will be presented on equipment and the ways in which it may affect teaching or performing skills.

TEACHING GUIDELINES

When teaching the various skills required for scuba diving safety, I follow a number of general guidelines. However, it is important to remember that there are very few absolutes in teaching, and you must always consider the student and the circumstances. The skills required and the performance standard which must be met will be determined by you, your student, the certifying agency, the planned activities, and the diving environment for which you are training.

General Considerations

- Be creative and encourage experimentation.
- Consider which skills are truly important for safety in the water.
- Consider which individual components of a skill are necessary for safety in the water.
- Encourage your students to develop individual styles which maximize comfort and convenience without compromising safety.
- Develop techniques which require the least amount of energy expenditure to accomplish the objective.
- Always be aware of the amount of energy your students expend.
- Always be aware of the effect of cold on energy levels and skill performance.
- In general, emphasize safe, proper performance over speed. In those instances where speed is necessary for safety, make sure the student understands why speed is a requirement.
- Encourage each student to become as independent as possible when performing skills. At the same time, be aware of circumstances which call for assistance from the buddy to accomplish the skill as quickly as possible. For example, I

have worked with students who are capable of removing and replacing their weight belt during pool training. However, these students required a great deal of time to perform the skill. During a cold water training dive, performing this skill with a heavy belt can contribute significantly to fatigue. I encourage these students to practice so that they maintain the ability to perform this skill. At the same time, if it became necessary to perform this skill during a dive, I would encourage them to ask for assistance. In this way they can avoid fatigue and enjoy the dive. For any diver, there can be a fine line between independence and stubborn refusal to accept reasonable amounts of assistance.

• Whenever possible, allow the student to develop an acceptable level of comfort by introducing skills in the shallow section of the pool. Initially, a student who is unable to stand unassisted may prefer the security of staying close to the side of the pool. Another technique for increasing feelings of security while underwater, is to position the student so she can reach the pool gutter or deck and pull herself to the surface (figure 4-1). Depending on the depth of the water, it may be necessary for the student to sit on a bench placed on the pool bottom. As the student gains skill and confidence, the training drills can be moved away from the security of the pool side.

FIGURE 4-1

MASK SKILLS

Many students with limited dexterity or range of motion will experience difficulty performing standard skills such as deliberately flooding and clearing or removing and replacing the mask. In some cases, the student will be able to perform some portion of the skill but not the entire skill. For example, a student with only one arm may find it easy to remove the mask and then hold it against his face. However, he may not be able to slip the strap over his head to complete the replacement process. When teaching mask skills, consider what is necessary to ensure the safety of the diver. Also consider which features of the mask will make it easier or more difficult for the student to handle the mask.

Equipment Considerations

* Masks with purge valves do not require use of the hands for clearing. However, the purge valve itself may block access to the nose pocket, making it difficult to equalize the ears.
* Students with limited dexterity may find it easier to handle wide mask straps as opposed to narrow or split straps.
* Wide straps may make it easier for a buddy to assist a diver to put on her mask.
* Low volume masks may make mask clearing or equalizing easier for students with impaired respiration.

Safety Considerations

* Students who experience difficulty clearing a mask must be able to breathe comfortably for extended periods of time from a regulator or snorkel, with a flooded mask or with no mask at all, while at the surface or underwater.
* Students who experience difficulty clearing a mask should be able to perform standard skills such as controlled ascents or sharing air with a flooded mask or with no mask at all.

Performing Mask Skills

A student who has the use of only one arm may be unable to manage the mask strap. However, she may be able to place the mask against her face, clear it of water, and hold it in position until her buddy is able to assist in positioning the strap. This skill is a big confidence builder for many students, and it also promotes the buddy team concept. A student with the use of only one arm may also be capable of putting on her mask and positioning the strap if there is a solid object against which she can press her face with the mask in place. For example, in the pool the student can place the mask against her face and then, with the mask in place, press the mask against the bottom of the pool or against her buddy. The mask will then be held in place while the student positions the strap.

In some cases, it may be necessary for the buddy to assist the student to place the mask against her face as well as to position the strap. If it is necessary to assist to this extent, the technique used will vary with the buddy team. One technique I have found useful is to place the mask against the diver's face and then slide the strap over the head. Performing the skill in this sequence prevents pulling the diver's hair or hood forward into the mask. The buddy may also find it helpful to place her hand between the strap and the diver's head, and to spread her fingers wide as she slides the strap over the diver's head. This will make it easier to prevent the strap from twisting as it is slipped over the diver's head. Figure 4-2 shows a diver with quadriplegia who is capable of clearing his own mask. However, he is not able to replace a mask which has come completely off. Figure 4-3 illustrates the buddy assisting the diver to replace his mask. Once the mask has been replaced, circumstances permitting, the diver should clear his mask unassisted.

It may be necessary to establish a signal which allows the diver or her buddy to communicate regarding the need or desire to clear the mask. Suggestions for a signal include eye blinks, head nods, or tapping the mask.

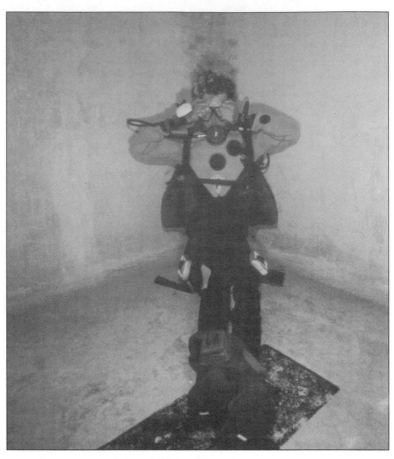

FIGURE 4-2

REGULATOR SKILLS

Divers with limited dexterity or range of motion may experience difficulty in manipulating regulator purge buttons or recovering lost regulators. It is important that the diver and her buddy be aware of the diver's abilities as well as her limitations. Loss of a regulator by a diver who is unable to recover the regulator can be fatal. Likewise, regulator malfunction or catastrophic air loss by a diver who is unable to propel herself through the water can also be fatal. Fortunately, such

FIGURE 4-3

events are rare. Nevertheless, it is vital that the dive buddy be extremely attentive at all times.

Equipment Considerations
*   Regulators should be high performance and breathe easily.
*   Regulators should be lightweight.
*   Regulators should be easy to clear.
*   Purge buttons should be easy to manipulate.
*   Custom or specialized mouthpieces may make it easier to retain the regulator.

Safety Considerations
*   A strap can help hold the regulator in or near the mouth, making it easier for the diver to retrieve the regulator.

- For some divers it may be advisable to use a full face mask or a mouthpiece which covers the entire mouth, such as those used in underwater communication systems.
- Remember that anything which makes it difficult to remove the regulator from the mouth will also make it difficult for the diver to share air from an alternate air source.
- Position the regulator on the diver's strong side. If the diver's left side is stronger, this will require a left hand second stage. As an alternative, a right hand second stage can be mounted on a 90 degree swivel.

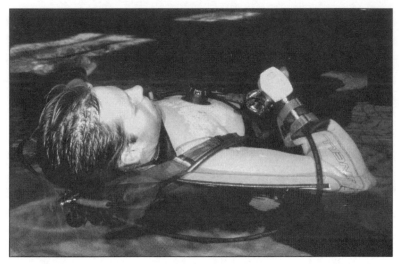

FIGURE 4-4

Performing Regulator Skills

Inability to retrieve the extra second stage may be an issue. It may be advisable for a diver with limited dexterity to strap the octopus to his forearm. Low profile second stages on a long hose work well for this application. Position the regulator on the diver's strong side and fasten it so that it can't slip or rotate. Velcro straps work well as fasteners, but be prepared to use two or three. Figure 4-4 shows a diver with an extra second stage strapped to his right forearm; notice the two straps holding it in place. Figure 4-5 shows the diver using the octopus while at depth. Before descending, the

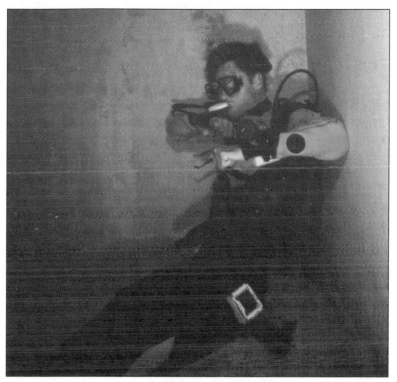

FIGURE 4-5

diver should check to ensure that the octopus is positioned so it is accessible. Also notice the weight belt across the diver's upper legs to hold him in position while he practices the skill.

BUOYANCY SKILLS

Many divers use their fins to control their rate of descent or ascent or to compensate for negative buoyancy. Obviously, this is not an option for divers who do not use fins. For these divers, buoyancy control takes on extra importance for two reasons. First, the diver must control her buoyancy to control her rate of descent or ascent. Second, a diver who does not use fins will expend a tremendous amount of energy to overcome negative buoyancy. These considerations are just as important to the buddy of a diver who is unable to operate her buoyancy compensator. A great deal of time should be set aside for practicing buoyancy control individually and as a team.

Equipment Considerations

- BC's with front adjustable straps and quick-release buckles may be easier for the diver to put on or take off. They may also make it easier for the buddy to help.
- Weight integrated buoyancy systems eliminate the necessity of dealing with a separate weight belt.
- BC's which allow one-handed control of both the low pressure inflator and the rapid exhaust facilitate buoyancy control for any diver.

Safety Considerations

- All BC's should be equipped with a low pressure inflation system for easy inflation and a rapid exhaust system for easy deflation.
- All BC controls should be as large and easy to manipulate as possible.
- As much as possible, the controls should be mounted on the diver's strong side.
- It is important to match the buoyancy characteristics of the diver and the buoyancy system. For instance, a back flotation system, which can force the diver onto her stomach at the surface, may not be appropriate for a diver who is unable to roll over in the water. Keep in mind that you must not sacrifice safety for comfort or convenience.

Performing Buoyancy Skills

It is critical that divers who do not use fins become proficient in controlling their buoyancy both by using the BC and regulating their breathing. Furthermore, divers who are unable to manipulate the BC controls must become proficient in controlling buoyancy by regulating their breathing. Ideally, divers who are unable to control the BC must always be capable of establishing positive buoyancy through some combination of breathing and body movement. In this way the

---

diver will always be able to ascend to the surface. If a diver who is unable to use the BC must perform an unassisted ascent, it must be treated as a positive buoyant ascent and the diver must not hold his breathe.

The use of lines can make controlled descents and ascents as well as safety stops much easier for any divers who do not use fins. However, a diver without fins, or a buddy team which includes a diver unable to use his BC, must demonstrate the ability to achieve neutral buoyancy at any point in the water column.

ENTRIES

The entry techniques used will vary with conditions and environment as well as with the diver. As always, the primary concern is the safety of the diver and her buddies.

General Considerations

- For many divers, the first issue is getting to the entry point. This may be accomplished by the diver herself without assistance or it may be necessary to assist the diver.
- The next decisions usually involve whether to put the gear on before or after entering the water and which type of entry to use. These decisions may also be influenced by the strength and stamina of the diver herself and the amount of assistance available.
- To avoid injury, a diver with no feeling or voluntary movement in her legs must make sure that her legs are controlled throughout the entry. This may be accomplished by the diver herself or by an assistant.

Entering from a low height

A diver who doesn't use fins, but has enough upper body strength and control to sit up, can use a seated face-first entry. To avoid landing on her face, the diver can twist to the side as she enters the water. The diver must make sure that her legs are floating free and are not caught on any obstructions such as pool gutters, ladders, lines, or kelp. It may be necessary to assist the diver to maintain her balance while

---

she is sitting and preparing to make her entry. It may also be appropriate to position a buddy in the water to assist the diver after her entry. If the diver puts on her gear prior to entry, make sure that the BC is inflated to provide positive buoyancy. Position the tank so that it will rest on the deck and support the diver. A tank which does not touch the deck may pull the diver over backwards. A tank which is too low may touch the deck before the diver touches the deck and actually push the diver forward. If the diver puts on her gear after entering the water, make sure that she has adequate buoyancy before putting on the weight system. Some divers may choose to perform a rear roll entry. Once again, it is important to make sure that her legs will not get caught or hung up on anything. This can be accomplished by having the diver cross her legs and pull them close to her body. The diver should hold onto her legs throughout the entry. Tank position can also be critical for this entry. The tank must be close enough to the edge that it will not get caught when the diver rolls backwards, but not so far over the edge that it will pull the diver over before she is ready. It may be necessary for a buddy to support the diver while she prepares for her entry.

Some divers are unable to enter the water on their own, and must be assisted into the water. This can be easily accomplished by positioning one assistant on the deck to support or lift the diver as necessary, and another in the water to receive the diver. In figure 4-6, the assistant in the water will receive the diver in a piggy-back position. The diver is carried away from the side of the pool and then released into the water. In some cases, the diver can simply be assisted to lean forward and plop into the water. Typically, this diver will put on her gear after entering the water. **In those situations where it is necessary to actually lift the diver over some obstruction, such as a pool gutter or boat rail, it is important that the diver's back be kept in as anatomically correct a position as possible. The assistants on deck must position themselves so that they can lower the diver into the water without hyperextending or arching the diver's back. Furthermore, the assistants should also avoid supporting the diver by**

FIGURE 4-6

her arms or shoulders. This can be accomplished by
the assistant wrapping her arms around the diver's
chest and pressing the diver into her own chest. Be
careful not to press too hard! The diver may be able to
assist by gripping the assistant's forearms. At the same
time, it is important that the assistant on the deck use
proper lifting techniques to avoid injuring her own
back. If the diver must be lifted into the water, it is easier on
the assistants if the diver puts on her gear after entering the
water.

Entering from a Beach or Shoreline

In some cases, divers who do not use fins are capable of
entering the water unassisted. Some divers will roll their
chairs into the water and then transfer into the water. Other
divers, preferring to keep their chairs out of the water, may
drag or "butt walk" themselves into the water. Butt walking
is a form of locomotion in which the person assumes a seated
position on the ground with her back to the direction she
wants to go. The diver then supports herself by her arms and

---

scoots her body backwards towards the water. If the diver is not capable of voluntary movement of the abdomen or torso, it will be necessary for her to reach behind herself and drag her body towards the water. This type of entry can be hard on wetsuits and gloves, as well as on the diver. Once again, the decision to put the gear on before or after entering the water is determined by the conditions and the strength and stamina of the diver.

Logistics can get a little more complex for divers who are unable to enter the water unassisted. In some situations it will be possible to roll the diver's chair to the water's edge and then assist the diver to transfer into the water. In other cases the diver must be carried across the beach and into the water. For these entries, effective use of assistants will help to minimize hassles. This is especially true when diving in cold water, since it is important to get moving as soon as possible to minimize concerns regarding hypothermia.

Basic Beach Entry Scenario

The following entry scenario outlines one plan for orchestrating a beach entry. This plan calls for a minimum of two assistants, at least one of whom can get the diver into the water unassisted.

1. Buddy 1 enters the water fully geared up and ready to go. This assistant will also have the diver's equipment in the water with her.
2. Buddy 2 helps the diver into the water and then returns her chair to a secure place.
3. While Buddy 2 is dealing with the chair, Buddy 1 helps the diver gear up. As soon as the diver is ready, both she and Buddy 1 begin to swim out to the dive site.
4. Meanwhile, after securing the chair Buddy 2 will gear up and catch up to the others to join them for the dive.

This plan has the advantage of minimizing the time spent floating around at the entry site. It has the disadvantage of requiring at least two assistants. Another disadvantage is that Buddy 2 must hurry to catch up with the other divers as

---

they swim out. Also, the dive team is separated for at least some portion of the surface swim.

Variation One

1. Buddy 1 enters the water geared up and ready to go. Buddy 1 also has with her the equipment for both the diver and Buddy 2.
2. Buddy 2 carries the diver into the water without using the chair.
3. Buddy 2 and the diver gear up, and the team swims out to the dive site.

This plan has the advantage of keeping the team together once they have entered the water. However, it has the disadvantage of requiring Buddy 2 to carry the diver across the beach.

Variation Two

1. The dive buddy assists the diver into the water.
2. After securing the chair, the buddy gears up herself and then brings the diver's gear out to her in the water. The diver then gears up, and the team swims out to the dive site.

This plan has the advantage of requiring only one buddy. However, it has the disadvantage of leaving the diver unattended in the water while she waits for her buddy to return with the gear. Another disadvantage is that the buddy must carry both sets of gear into the water. Carrying two sets of gear simultaneously requires a certain amount of strength. Carrying the two sets out one after the other adds time to the entry. It also increases the amount of time the diver is in the water without a buddy.

Variation Three

1. The buddy assists the diver into the water.
2. The buddy brings the diver's gear to her in the water.

---

3. The buddy returns to the beach to gear up and then re-enters the water.
4. The dive team swims out to the dive site.

The advantage of this plan over variation two is that the buddy only carries one set of gear at a time. The disadvantages of this variation are that more time is spent floating in the entry area and that the diver and buddy are separated for a greater length of time.

Variation Four
1. The buddy puts both sets of gear in the water first.
2. The buddy carries the diver into the water.
3. The divers gear up and swim out to the dive site.

The advantages of this variation are minimum time spent floating at the entry site and minimum time spent apart. The disadvantages are that it requires calm water with no current so that the gear will not float away. Another option is to secure the gear so that it will not float away, but this requires more equipment and preparation.

EXITS
Just as with entries, many divers with disabilities will be capable of exiting the water unassisted. Other divers with disabilities will require help. The exit technique used will be determined by the conditions, the diver himself and the amount of assistance available.

General Considerations
Frequently, it is a good idea for a diver with special needs to remove heavy equipment prior to exiting the water.

Exiting from a Swimming Pool
Without Assistance
Many divers with disabilities are capable of exiting from a pool without assistance. Typically, these divers find it easiest to exit at the corners, as this allows them to position their

FIGURE 4-7

FIGURE 4-8

FIGURE 4-9

FIGURE 4-10

FIGURE 4-11

hands to get maximum leverage (see figures 4-7, 4-8, and 4-9). Some divers may prefer to exit with their back to the side of the pool, while others may choose to face the side of the pool while exiting. Figures 4-10 and 4-11 show a diver with Spastic cerebral palsy facing the side of the pool as he exits. Notice how stiff the diver is and the effort required to perform the exit. Regardless of the technique used, it may be necessary to pad the edge of the pool and the deck itself.

Exiting into a Small Boat Without Assistance

When exiting the water into a small boat, it may be possible to create a 90 degree angle by using the outboard engine and the transom itself. In the case of an inflatable, it may be possible to use the transom and a portion of the pontoon.

Exiting from Deep Water with Assistance

Divers who are unable to exit without assistance must be lifted from the water. This can be done with Buddy 1 in the boat or on the pool deck and Buddy 2 in the water. After all heavy gear has been removed, Buddy 1 reaches under the diver's

FIGURE 4-12

arms and around his chest. Buddy 2 then positions himself so that his shoulders are under the back of the diver's upper legs (the hamstrings). As Buddy 1 lifts from above, Buddy 2 pushes up from the water. By working together, the lifting team can ensure that at no point is the diver's weight supported completely by Buddy 1's grip on the diver's chest. Figure 4-12 shows a buddy team assisting a diver from the water. Notice how the assistant is gripping the forearms of the diver.

Exiting onto a Beach

As with entries, the objective here is to manage equipment transfers effectively. A little advance organization will minimize energy expenditure as well as time spent floating in the water. Keep in mind, that on occasion, floating in the water will be a very enjoyable experience for a diver with a disability. However, at other times, such as when hypothermia is a concern, it may be beneficial to remove the diver from the water as quickly as possible.

Basic Beach Exit Scenario

Orchestrating the exit can begin as soon as you start swimming back to the beach.

1. If it is possible, send Buddy 1 ahead to the beach. This person can exit the water, remove his gear, bring the diver's chair to the water and prepare to assist with the exit.
2. When the diver arrives at the exit site, the diver can remove his gear and give it to Buddy 2.
3. Buddy 2 will remain with the gear while Buddy 1 assists the diver to exit the water.
4. Buddy 1 can then return to Buddy 2 and help to transport the diver's gear out of the water. (If Buddy 2 has had his Wheaties that day, he may choose to carry out both sets of gear without assistance. I like to wait.)

This plan gets the diver out of the water with minimal waiting and at no point is the diver left alone in the water.

Variation One

If it is not necessary to get a chair for the diver, the buddy team may choose to swim in together. On reaching the exit point, Buddy 1 and the diver will remove their gear and leave it with Buddy 2. After assisting the diver with the exit, Buddy 1 will return to assist Buddy 2 with the equipment. (Remember that you have Buddy 1's gear, so if you wait long enough he will come back.)

The advantage of this plan is that the dive team remains together throughout the dive. This plan also gets the diver out of the water with minimal waiting.

Variation Two

In this scenario, only one buddy is available to assist.

1. The dive buddy swims ahead to exit, removes his gear, gets the chair and prepares to assist with the exit.
2. The diver arrives at the dive site and removes his gear. The buddy removes the diver's gear from the water and comes back to assist the diver with the exit.

The advantage of this plan is that it allows the diver to exit the water with minimal waiting. The disadvantage is that the dive team is separated for some period of time. **Obviously, for this plan even to be considered, both members of the dive team must be capable of acting independently in the water at all times.**

Variation Three

1. The dive team remains together as they swim to the exit point.
2. On arriving at the exit site, the diver is assisted to the beach by a buddy. The diver then waits while the buddy goes to get the chair or removes gear from the water as necessary. Once again, it may be helpful to have some means of tethering the gear in the water, so you can keep the gear out of the sand or dirt until you are ready to transport it across the beach.

The advantage of this plan is that the dive team remains together throughout the dive. The disadvantage is that the diver must wait at the exit site until equipment logistics have been dealt with.

SELF-RESCUE SKILLS

For any diver, self-rescue skills are the most important of all emergency diving skills. The extent to which a diver can perform self rescue will be determined by the diver's physical ability and, to some extent, by the divers equipment.

General Considerations

- Some divers may be unable to wave their arms in the commonly recognized distress signal. For these divers, audible signaling devices are extremely important.
- Whenever possible, the diver's weight system should be arranged so that the weight can be dumped by the diver using a quick release.
- A diver who is unable to control her BC, should always be able to establish positive buoyancy by some combination of breathing and body movements.
- A diver who has difficulty operating the BC controls or ditching a weight system without assistance, but who can activate a CO_2 cartridge, should consider a BC which incorporates a CO_2 cartridge.
- A diver who is unable to swim to his buddy or to the surface, should consider carrying a redundant scuba system.
- A diver who is unable to roll over from front to back, should consider a BC which will float him on his back when at the surface.
- A diver who is unable to clear or replace his mask unassisted, must be comfortable breathing for several minutes with no mask or with a flooded mask.
- The ability to move through the water as efficiently as possible is an important aspect of self rescue. As an instructor, you should learn as much as possible about proper stroke techniques for a diver who swims with his upper body. Unfortunately, it is beyond the scope of this guide to discuss the mechanics of arm strokes for swimming either on the surface or at depth. Furthermore, the wide range of physical abilities you will encounter will call for modifying any stroke pattern to accommodate the students. Keep in mind that even students with very limited range of motion can learn to scull effectively with their hands, significantly enhancing their safety in the water. One good source of information regarding stroke mechanics is _Swimming & Diving_ which is available through the American Red Cross.
- **A diver who is unable to perform basic self-rescue skills such as ditching his weights or inflating his BC must make sure that his buddy understands the**

---

level of buddy support necessary to conduct a safe dive. **It is equally important that the diver satisfy himself that his buddy has the skills, knowledge and physical ability to provide adequate buddy support.** As the instructor it is your responsibility to educate the diver so that he is aware of the questions to ask a potential dive buddy and can evaluate the answers he receives. As with any dive team, the divers should evaluate each other's experience, knowledge of the dive environment, knowledge of the planned dive activities and comfort level with each other as a dive buddy. Practically speaking, these questions are no different than those that should be asked by any diver.

BUDDY RESCUE SKILLS

Whenever possible, a diver should develop the skills necessary to assist her buddy in the event of an emergency. Many divers with disabilities are fully capable of providing buddy rescue support. Others may be capable of limited buddy rescue support or may require minor modifications to their equipment or technique.

General Considerations

It is important that each member of the dive team be aware of the rescue capability of the other team members.

- Some divers may lack the strength or stamina to tow a buddy for even a short distance. However, these divers may be capable of establishing positive buoyancy and providing rescue breathing for their buddies. These divers must be cautioned to operate within their limits and not exhaust themselves to the point of becoming victims themselves.
- Some divers may be unable to wave their arms in the commonly recognized distress signal. For these divers, audible signaling devices are extremely important.
- As with any skill, be creative and focus on developing effective techniques for buddy rescue.

FIGURE 4-13

FIGURE 4-14

Tired Diver Assists

- A diver who swims with his upper body can tow his buddy by grasping the buddy with one hand and performing a sidestroke or modified backstroke with the other arm, as in figure 4-13.
- A diver who swims with his upper body can carry a rescue line with quick release fasteners at each end. The line can be attached to the buddy and to the diver, allowing the diver to swim with both arms. This technique will also work for a diver who only has the use of one arm. It is important that the line have a quick release mechanism so the diver can easily disengage from his buddy if necessary.
- A diver who swims with his upper body can use the fin push technique to assist a tired diver, as shown in figure 4-14.
- A diver who swims with his upper body can hook his legs onto the diver needing assistance, keeping both arms free for swimming. Another option is to have the tired diver hold onto the legs of the rescuer (see figure 4-15). In either situation the rescuer must be extremely careful, as he is in contact with a diver who may panic.

FIGURE 4-15

Underwater Rescue

A diver who swims with his upper body can raise an unresponsive diver from depth to the surface. Keep in mind that because the rescuer doesn't use fins it is likely that he will control the ascent using either his or the victim's BC as a lifting device. To avoid uncontrolled ascents, it is important that the diver be capable of maintaining appropriate ascent rates throughout the rescue.

FIGURE 4-16

Rescue Breathing

A diver who swims with his upper body can provide rescue breathing for his buddy. However, a diver with no voluntary control of the leg or abdominal muscles may be unable to maintain a stable position while performing rescue breathing. This diver may need to use techniques such as mouth-to-snorkel breathing. Jill Robinson and Dale Fox have suggested a pocket mask with a length of tubing attached. This diver may actually use the person he is rescuing as a means of support while performing rescue breathing or removing gear. The rescuer in figure 4-16 has had both legs amputated at

FIGURE 4-17

FIGURE 4-18

FIGURE 4-19

FIGURE 4-20

FIGURE 4-21

the hips, and the rescuer shown in figure 4-17 has paraplegia. Nevertheless, by pulling the victim's body close to their own, each rescuer is able to maintain an upright position and provide effective rescue breathing.

Divers who experience stiffness of the limbs may find it difficult to achieve an upright position in the water, especially when wearing a wetsuit but no weight belt. Notice in figure 4-18 the diver is in a horizontal position at the surface. While the diver is able to get close enough to provide rescue breathing, it is an awkward process. By contrast in figures 4-19, 4-20, and 4-21, the diver is wearing a weight belt and BC and is able to achieve an upright position, making it easier to provide effective rescue breathing. Notice the various arm positions as the diver experiments to find the most effective technique.

A diver who swims with his upper body may be unable to swim while performing rescue breathing for a buddy.

EQUIPMENT HANDLING SKILLS

For many divers with special needs, the most difficult aspect of scuba is handling heavy, bulky gear. This is especially true out of the water where the equipment is heaviest. Also, impaired mobility is often most pronounced when out of the water. At the same time, the more the diver is responsible for her equipment, the more involved she will become in the dive. As always, each diver should be encouraged to achieve the maximum level of independence.

General Considerations

- Handling equipment can require significant amounts of time and energy. The diver should be aware of the trade-off between accepting full responsibility for handling her own equipment and exhausting herself to the point of creating an unsafe situation during the dive.
- The diver should be completely satisfied with the performance and configuration of her equipment prior to entering the water.

Assembly and Disassembly

Encouraging divers to practice the buddy system while handling equipment can save a great deal of time and energy. It will also promote teamwork and the concept of the buddy team, both of which are important aspects of scuba for divers with special needs.

A diver who uses a wheelchair may assemble or disassemble her gear while sitting in her chair, or she may choose to get out of her chair and sit on the ground. Should the diver choose to remain in her chair, she may find it easier to work on her equipment if it is placed on a bench or table, as shown in figures 4-22 and 4-23. Raising the equipment helps avoid the awkward positions which may occur when sitting in a chair and handling equipment which is on the ground. Figures 4-24, 4-25, 4-26, and 4-27 illustrate the process of lifting a tank from the ground while sitting in a chair, as does figure 4-28. As you can imagine, this can be an awkward process

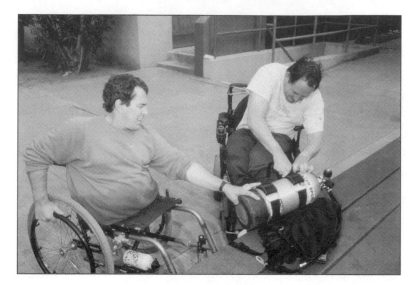

FIGURE 4-22

FIGURE 4-23

FIGURE 4-24

FIGURE 4-25

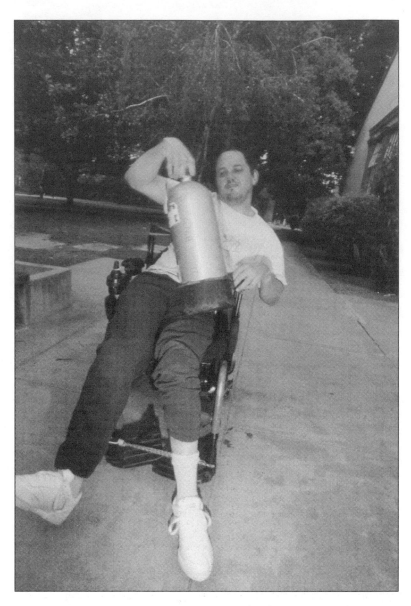

FIGURE 4-26

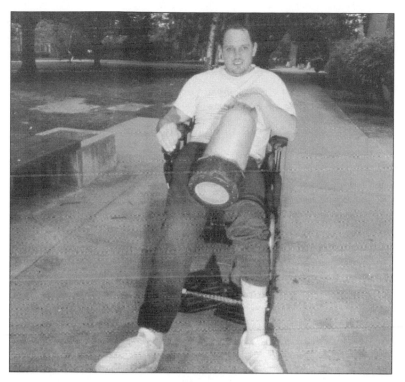

FIGURE 4-27

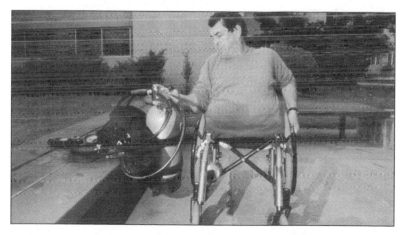

FIGURE 4-28

FIGURE 4-29

requiring strength on the part of the diver. By comparison, figure 4-29 shows that two divers working as a buddy team make the job much easier. Whether the diver remains in her chair or transfers to the ground, make sure she has adequate clear space in which to work.

A diver may be unable to assemble or disassemble her equipment. Nevertheless, it is still the diver's responsibility to ensure that her equipment is properly assembled and in good working order. The diver must be thoroughly familiar with procedures for assembling and testing equipment. Furthermore, the diver should observe the person who is assembling and testing her equipment and be prepared to correct any errors or unsatisfactory situations. It is a good idea to test the diver by occasionally making a mistake during the assembly process. If the diver doesn't notice and correct you, it is important that you point out the error and the fact that she missed it. Make sure to correct the mistake before starting the dive.

Putting on and Removing Gear

- Frequently, divers with impaired strength, mobility, range of motion or stamina will find it easiest to put on and remove gear while in the water.
- Buoyancy Compensators with front adjustable straps and quick release buckles are usually the easiest and quickest to put on and take off.

Putting on Gear with Assistance

A diver who is unable to put on her gear unassisted may find it easiest to lie on her back in the water while the buddies float her BC up against her back. When the BC is first floated up against the diver's back, the quick-release straps should be undone. Once the BC is properly positioned, the straps can be fastened. If the BC does not have quick-release buckles, it may be advisable to start with the BC under the water and beneath the mid section or lower body of the diver. The diver should allow her arms to float naturally. The buddies can then slide the scuba unit up the diver's body, pulling the diver's arms through the arm openings of the BC. This sequence helps avoid twisting the diver's arms, shoulders or body. If there is any concern about dunking the diver, it is a good idea to place her regulator in her mouth and have her wear her mask. Keep in mind that because the diver is on her back, the tank may sag away from her body and pull on the regulator, so it may be a good idea to have a long hose on the diver's regulator. Also keep in mind that the diver is lying on her back and may be staring directly into the sun. It may increase the diver's comfort to wear a hat or sunglasses until it is actually time to descend and start the dive. Also, because she is lying on her back, the diver may be unable to see what her buddies are doing. It may increase her comfort level if her buddies keep her informed about what is happening.

Putting on Gear without Assistance

A diver who is capable of handling her own gear in the water may experience difficulty maintaining her balance if she lacks control of her torso, abdomen or legs. This diver might experience difficulty putting on her scuba unit using tradi-

---

FIGURE 4-30

FIGURE 4-31

tional techniques such as the "over the head method." If a diver has difficulty maintaining her balance, it is important to keep the equipment and the diver's center of gravity as low as possible. In figures 4-30, 4-31 and 4-32, notice how the diver stays low in the water.

Another technique which has proved workable is to lie on the tank and then roll or spin into the scuba unit. This technique requires little strength or balance and provides flotation throughout the skill. The following sequence seems to work well for most divers.

1. Inflate the BC just enough to ensure it will float. The tank should be beneath the water and the backpack side of the BC should be facing up at the surface.
2. Position the BC so that the bottom of the tank is at the diver's chest. The diver will be facing the tank.
3. Have the diver reach across her chest with one hand and put her arm through the arm opening of her BC. For example, if the diver is facing the end of the tank, she must reach across her body and the BC to put her right arm through the right arm opening. If the diver does start with her right arm, this will allow her to breathe on her regulator throughout the maneuver. However, based on strength, range of motion or other considerations, it may be advisable to start with the left arm.
4. Have the diver roll onto the BC so that she is lying on her back with her arm through the opening. If the diver placed her right arm through the opening prior to rolling on to the BC, her right arm should still be through the BC, and her left arm should be free.
5. At this point, the diver can put her free arm through the appropriate arm opening. The diver may find this easier to do if she slides the BC down her body towards her waist. This will allow her to slip her arm through the BC opening by reaching down towards her waist. This movement is typically more comfortable than reaching back over the shoulder or behind the back.
6. The diver should now be in the BC and can adjust straps, buckles and hoses as necessary.

FIGURE 4-32

Common errors when performing this technique include:

- Overinflating the BC so that it is difficult to maneuver.
  Sometimes watching the student work against an overin-
  flated BC is like watching a wrestling match. Unfortu-

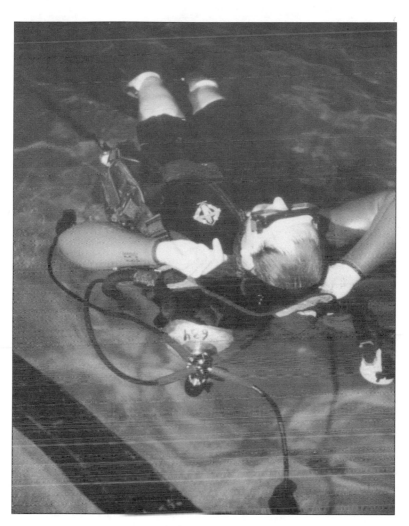

FIGURE 4-33

nately, the student doesn't always win. Overinflation also causes the BC to press tightly against the student's back as she is lying on the BC. This makes it difficult to slide the BC up and down the body as the diver completes the maneuver.

- Not sliding the BC down the body as the diver puts the second arm through the arm opening. Failure to reposition

---

FIGURE 4-34

the BC can frequently lead to the diver assuming an uncomfortable position as she attempts to position the second arm. Notice in figures 4-33 and 4-34 that the diver has not positioned the scuba unit at the lower body, and so must reach up and back to find the arm openings of the BC. It is typically much less awkward to reach down toward the waist. Occasionally, the diver's contortions can cause her to dunk her face or twist onto her back, so it may be advisable to have her breathe on the regulator as soon as possible.

Removing Scuba

- As with any diver, it is important to make sure that the diver will have adequate support or buoyancy prior to removing the BC. It may be necessary to remove the weight system prior to removing the BC.
- It is generally easiest to release the cummerbund, waist straps, chest straps and shoulder straps while the student is floating on her back at the surface. The scuba unit can then be submerged and moved away from the diver. Make

sure that no straps, buckles or hoses are caught on the diver, especially in areas where she has no sensation.

BUDDY TECHNIQUES

When diving with divers with special needs, the buddy system becomes even more important than in traditional diving. Proper buddy techniques are not only an essential aspect of diving enjoyment, they are a vital component of dive safety. It is crucial that all members of the dive team understand the abilities and limitations and roles of each diver. Furthermore, each diver must feel comfortable and confident as a member of the team. This section will discuss dive team composition as well as various techniques and concerns related to buddy teams which include a diver with special needs.

Dive Team Composition

Divers with special needs and their buddies must consider the composition of the dive team very carefully. In particular, the divers must be aware of the availability of rescue support for each member of the team. Many divers with disabilities are not only capable of diving independently but can also provide rescue support for a dive buddy in need. Practically speaking, for these divers there are no special considerations with regard to dive team composition. However, not all divers are capable of rescuing themselves, much less their buddies.

The primary concern for divers who are incapable of rescuing a buddy is whether or not they are capable of performing self-rescue. Divers who can rescue themselves are advised to dive with two buddies, both of whom are capable of rescuing themselves or a buddy. In such a dive team, no matter who may require rescue, one member of the team can provide buddy rescue while the other member can perform self-rescue as necessary. For example, consider a team in which divers A and B can perform buddy rescue and diver C is capable of self rescue. If diver A gets in trouble, diver B can provide support and diver C can take care of herself. If diver C gets in trouble, either A or B can provide support.

FIGURE 4-35

In the event that a diver is incapable of performing self-rescue, it is recommended that the diver team up with divers of higher levels of experience and training. At a minimum, at least one of the buddies should have training in scuba rescue. Aside from learning actual rescue techniques, rescue divers also receive training in recognizing potential problems and preventing the need for an actual rescue. Even greater safety is provided if one of the buddies has experience and training in diving leadership. Instructors, assistant instructors, divemasters, or dive guides often have wide experience in anticipating, recognizing, preventing, or controlling the difficulties encountered by divers of all levels of experience and ability .

General Considerations
- The buddy of any diver must be fully aware of any assistance or accommodation the diver is likely to need. The dive buddy's knowledge, skills, and physical condition must be equal to the task of providing assistance as necessary. If either diver has any doubt, the team should sit out the dive.
- The buddy of any diver should be completely familiar with the manner in which the diver has set up his equipment.

FIGURE 4-36

- The buddy of a diver who swims with his upper body, as in figure 4-35, must maintain enough distance to allow the diver a full arm sweep. This will allow the diver to swim without interference, and will prevent the buddy from being swiped across the mask or regulator.
- If the diver is weaker on one side of his body, it may be necessary for the buddy to position himself on the weaker side of the diver. In figure 4-36, the diver's left arm is at full extension. Also notice the position of the left hand. This diver may be more likely to require assistance for tasks involving the left side of the body.
- Depending on the ability of the diver, it may be necessary for the buddy to remain in physical contact at all times.
- Many divers with special needs will not have a great deal of strength or stamina. It is important that the dive buddy match his pace to the pace of the diver. When in doubt, slow down! Fatigue or cold may come on very suddenly for some divers, and it is important that they have the physical reserves to deal with any unexpected stress during the dive. On the other hand, moving too slowly can actually cause divers to feel cold, so you must find a good balance between pace and energy expenditure.

FIGURE 4-37

Acting as a Buddy for a Diver Unable to Dive Independently

• Remain in contact with that diver at all times.

• If the diver is unable to control her buoyancy, it is vital that the dive buddy be capable of controlling both her own buoyancy and that of the diver. This requires excellent personal buoyancy skills as well as familiarity with the diver's equipment.

• Ultimately, you and the diver must decide on the safest state of buoyancy for the diver.

Personally, I prefer to have the diver neutral or slightly buoyant at all times. This can mean extra work for the buddy as he may have to physically hold the diver down. However, it also means that no matter what happens the diver should be able to get to the surface. These divers must be skilled at controlling buoyancy by regulating the volume of air in their lungs. These divers must also be skilled in proper breathing during emergency ascents. Notice in figure 4-37 the diver is neutral and upright.

FIGURE 4-38

From this position the diver is able to initiate an unassisted ascent.

- If a diver is unable to clear his ears or mask without assistance, the buddy must maintain eye contact continuously throughout the dive. In this situation, one option is to swim on your back with the diver horizontal above you so that you are essentially belly-to-belly. Another option is to position yourself slightly ahead of the diver and swim backwards as you tow him.
- A diver who is unable to swim must be towed through the water by the buddy or buddies. This can be accomplished in a number of ways:
1. One buddy can swim at the head and upper body of the diver, while the other buddy controls the diver's feet and legs, as shown in figure 4-38. This requires teamwork but has the advantage of sharing the workload. This technique can also make it difficult to spot interesting things during the dive as both buddies are constantly occupied with the buddy. In some cases it is easiest to have the buddies on opposite sides of the diver's body. In other cases the buddy working at the diver's upper body may find it easier to swim above the diver, almost as if he were riding the diver's tank. This position allows the buddy to

FIGURE 4-39

grab the diver's BC on both sides of the tank and provides
good control of the diver's trim. However, being above the
diver can interfere with the buddy's kick and also increase
the difficulty of communicating with the diver.

2. One buddy can take sole responsibility for towing the diver
   while the other acts as a spotter or navigator. In this situation, it may actually be easier for the buddy doing the towing to keep the diver in a vertical position as they move

through the water, as shown in figure 4-39. I have found it easier to swim behind the diver holding onto the cylinder valve. If you choose to do this, be careful not to keep nudging the tank valve, as it is possible to nudge it to the point of restricting air flow. Also keep in mind that you will be unable to maintain eye contact with the diver, so you must devise some signaling system. I have found it works well to tap the diver on the head. If he nods yes, he is O.K.. Any other response is not O.K. Make sure that the diver is capable of letting you know immediately if he is in trouble or needs assistance. When using touch signals, be aware of any areas of the body where the diver has no sensation.

WEIGHTING

Many divers with disabilities will demonstrate unusual buoyancy characteristics. They may also be unable to use leg or abdominal muscles to achieve proper balance and trim in the water. For these divers, how they distribute their weights may be just as important as the total amount of weight they wear.

General Considerations

Observing the student in the pool while she is wearing full open water equipment, except the weight belt, may give you an indication of her buoyancy characteristics. It will also give you and her an idea of her ability to compensate for the effects of the equipment. Based on these observations, you can make an initial estimate of how much weight she will need and where to position the weights. You should also keep in mind that in some cases extra weight may not be the answer. For instance, floating arms are most noticeable when adding air to a dry suit, and this problem can be addressed with an exhaust valve located in the forearm of the suit.

Frequently, weights must be placed in unconventional locations. For instance, a diver who has little no control of her arms may find that they have a tendency to float over her head. This diver may find it desirable to position some weights on her forearm to counteract this excessive buoyancy. At the same time, care must be taken not to adversely affect the diver's trim or inhibit her ability to use her arms. Furthermore, be careful not to get so caught up in placing weights to accommodate specific buoyancy characteristics that you actually overweight the diver. **It is important to check the diver's buoyancy with all weights and equipment in place. Also, make sure that one quick release will dump enough weight to provide positive buoyancy.**

If a diver shows a tendency to roll to one side, it may not be appropriate simply to place a counterweight on the other side of the body directly opposite the area which initiates the roll. In fact, doing so may affect other areas of the body. It may actually be necessary to shift or position weight on the opposite side of the body and to move it in the direction of the head or the feet. Snuggling the weights tightly at the diver's side may also reduce the tendency to roll. However, it is important to avoid excessive pressure over bony areas of the body. Also, during the early phases of training, it is a good idea to remove hard, bulky equipment, such as weight belts, at 15-20 minute intervals and inspect the skin.

When swimming on their stomachs, divers with atrophied lower limbs can be forced into a head-down trim due to positive buoyancy of their legs. Weights placed on the ankles or legs can counteract the buoyancy of the diver's legs. However too much weight can pull the legs too far down, causing excessive drag. Also, these weights can cause the legs to drag at depth as the diver's buoyancy changes. It is very helpful to use weights which can be repositioned or even removed. If the diver chooses to remove the weights, they can be carried by the diver or the buddy.

The size and position of the diver's tank can have tremendous impact on a swimming diver's trim. A tank worn too high on the back can force the diver into a head-down orientation, while a tank worn too low can force the diver into a head-up position. Take the time to experiment with different tank sizes and positions. The weight of the tank can also make it difficult for a diver unable to use her leg or abdomi-

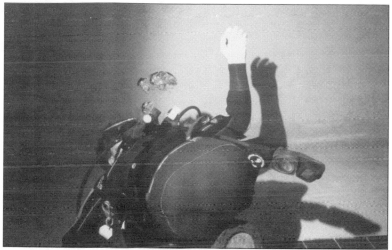

FIGURE 4-40

nal muscles to maintain balance in an upright position. Frequently the tank will pull the diver onto her back. If the diver has sufficient strength and range of motion, she may be able to pull herself to a more upright position in the water by grabbing the exposure suit material at her upper legs and pulling. It may be necessary to grab the sides or back of the legs as opposed to the top of the thighs. By grabbing the back of the legs, she may be able to pull her legs down as she pulls her torso forward and up.

A diver who is unable to maintain an upright position in the water may find it difficult or uncomfortable to lift her head out of the water to listen to discussions at the surface. This diver may find it helpful to have a small float at the surface to support her head and enable her to hear what is being said. Another solution is to place counterweights on the front of the BC. Often, a counterweight combined with some air in the BC will act to hold the student upright. The size and position of the weight will vary with the diver. It is important to determine if the diver is capable of rolling over onto her back without assistance, as this is an important aspect of self-rescue. It is also important to make sure that the diver is capable of dealing with mask, regulator, buoyancy and other skills while lying on her back.

The diver may also be susceptible to being pulled onto her back while underwater. Notice in figure 4-40 that the diver has been pulled over and is actually lying on the tank. This situation was resolved by placing weights at the lower front portion of the diver's body. This stabilized the diver, making it much easier to achieve an upright position. By contrast, the diver in figures 4-41 and 4-42 found that adding counterweights to the front of the BC made it possible to attain an upright position. In some cases, it takes a combination of factors to achieve the desired trim. In order for the diver in figure 4-43 to achieve the vertical position desired, the following combination was used: ankle weights, a counterweight at the front of the BC, and weights strapped to each forearm. The diver is wearing a weight integrated, back inflation BC.

Many instructors prefer to conduct skills training with both the student and the instructor in a sitting or kneeling position. Unfortunately, students with rigid muscles or excessively buoyant lower limbs may find it uncomfortable or even impossible to sit or kneel. As the instructor, you must be comfortable conducting skills training while sitting, kneeling, lying or even floating vertically in the water.

A student with excessively buoyant legs can achieve a vertical position in the water by placing weights on her ankles to pull her feet down. The student can then control her position by holding onto an ascent line, the bottom of a ladder, a pole lowered into the pool, or the side of the pool itself. Ultimately, the student should be able to control her position by establishing neutral buoyancy.

In order to sit on the bottom, a student with excessively buoyant legs can use ankle weights or a weight belt draped across the thighs, shins, or ankles to control the legs while in a sitting position. Extra stability can be provided by positioning the student in the corner of the pool. This will prevent the tank from pulling the student backwards and at the same

FIGURE 4-41

FIGURE 4-42

FIGURE 4-43

Teaching Techniques

FIGURE 4-44

FIGURE 4-45

time prevent side-to-side slipping. In figure 4-44, a weight belt has been draped across the diver's lower legs to prevent the feet from slipping. However, notice that the diver is slipping down almost onto his back. By contrast, in figure 4-45 the weights are draped across the hips, allowing the feet to

FIGURE 4-46

float out of control, tipping the diver backwards. The best results have been achieved by placing weights at both the hips and ankles. As illustrated in figure 4-45, this enables the diver to maintain an upright position. **Be aware that placing the weights in this configuration may make it** impossible for the diver to get to the surface without assistance. When using this configuration, extreme caution must be exercised and the diver can never be left unattended.

If it is not practical to sit in a corner, the student can sit leaning against the wall, or assistants can be positioned to provide support as appropriate.

DESCENTS/ASCENTS

During descent or ascent, most divers find it more comfortable to remain in a vertical position. Unfortunately, a diver with no control of his legs may find that his legs float, forcing him onto his back. Also, the weight of the tank will act to pull him onto his back. Keep in mind that this can also become a safety issue. Some models of BC make it difficult for a diver who is upside down to dump air quickly from the BC. This means that a diver who is upside down or on his back and adds too much air to the BC during descent risks an uncontrolled ascent. Depending on the circumstances, this situation can be dealt with in a number of ways.

General Considerations

• A diver who doesn't use fins must control his rate of descent with his BC.
• Maintaining a vertical position during descent usually provides the greatest level of comfort and control for the diver.
• A diver who is likely to be pulled onto his back during descent should consider a BC which will allow him to dump air from a head-down position.
• Descent/Ascent lines can provide a means of controlling the rate of descent or ascent.

Descents

A Diver Capable of Controlling His Own Buoyancy

• A diver who is able to control his own buoyancy may wear ankle weights during descent or ascent. Frequently, these weights will cause the diver's legs to drag along the bot-

FIGURE 4-47

FIGURE 4-48

FIGURE 4-49

tom while at depth, so it is helpful to use weights which can be easily removed or repositioned during the dive. The weights can then be carried by the buddy, reattached to the diver at a different location, or even left at the descent/ascent point. Of course this means that you must be able to find the same ascent point at the end of the dive. In figure 4-47 the diver is using ankle weights to achieve a vertical position for descent. Once at the bottom, the diver removes the weights to prevent his feet from dragging along the bottom (figure 4-48).

- The dive buddy can also submerge and hold the diver's legs down. The diver should not pull the diver down by his legs but should simply prevent them from floating up as the diver controls his own descent. This requires teamwork as well as excellent buoyancy control on the part of the buddy.

- A diver who is pulled onto his back during descent may find it easier to regain control by rolling onto his stomach instead of fighting to regain an upright position.

A Diver Incapable of Controlling His Own Buoyancy

- Ankle weights can be placed on the diver to pull the feet down and get the diver in a vertical position. The buddy will then control the buoyancy of both divers during descent and ascent. I find it easiest to establish control using my fins and the BC of the diver. Notice in figure 4-49 that the buddy is maintaining eye contact as the descent is initiated.
- The dive buddy can force the diver's legs into a vertical position by using his own legs to hold down the diver's legs. The buddy will then control both his and the diver's buoyancy. This can be a little cozy, and it takes practice, but it works well. This technique avoids having to deal with the ankle weights at the bottom.
- If two buddies are available, one buddy can submerge to control the diver's feet and legs, while the other buddy assists the diver with the BC. Once again, this can get cozy and it requires teamwork between the two buddies. However, it avoids dealing with the ankle weights at depth. Notice in figure 4-50 that the buddy at the upper body is behind the diver. As the descent takes place, this buddy must move to the front and maintain eye contact with the diver.
- If the diver is unable to control his arms, it may be necessary to capture the diver's arms between the bodies of the diver and the buddy. This is particularly true when the diver is wearing a dry suit and the arms fill with air. However, be aware that if the exhaust valve is located on the arm of the suit, it may be necessary to raise the arm to dump air.

FIGURE 4-50

Ascents

A Diver Capable of Controlling His Own Buoyancy

A diver who swims with his upper body is capable of swimming to the surface. However, because his hands and arms are occupied with swimming it may be difficult for him to watch his gauges to monitor his ascent. This diver must either mount his console where it will remain in sight without holding it, or control his ascent rate using his BC and breath control. The diver must be capable of performing a safety stop.

A Diver Incapable of Controlling His Own Buoyancy

- When the divers must perform the ascent as a team, the team must be capable of controlling the rate of ascent and performing a safety stop. I find it easiest to control the rate of ascent using the diver's BC and my fins.
- An ascent line can be extremely helpful in these situations. However, as there is no guarantee that an ascent line will always be available, the diver or dive team must be capable of controlling free ascents and performing safety stops.
- As on descent, it may be necessary to control the diver's legs during ascent, and once again it is important to be aware of the potential for an uncontrolled ascent. The control techniques used on ascent are typically the same as those used on descent.

OUT-OF-AIR SITUATIONS

Fortunately, divers do not run out of air very often. However, it does happen, and every diver and dive team should be prepared to respond to an out-of-air situation. This section will discuss techniques for sharing air.

General Considerations

The diver who is out of air may have weak facial muscles and be unable to establish a strong grip with his teeth. Also, the diver who is out of air may be unable to use his hands to help secure the regulator in his mouth. Therefore, it is important that the dive buddy not make sudden moves that might yank the regulator out of the diver's mouth.

During a shared-air ascent, it is possible that the diver with air remaining is also close to being out of air. In such a situation, it is important to use the remaining air wisely. When possible, it may be appropriate for the diver who uses fins to swim the buddy team up at a controlled rate of ascent. If the diver who does not use fins controls the ascent, she may find it necessary to use either her or her buddy's BC for lift. If so, she should add air to the BC as sparingly as possible for two reasons. First, as much air as possible should be conserved for breathing. Second, having the minimum amount of air necessary in the BC allows the diver the best chance of controlling the rate of ascent.

CHAPTER SUMMARY

As scuba instructors, it is our job to assist our students in acquiring the knowledge and skills necessary to dive in safety and comfort. Exactly what those skills and knowledge entail, and the standard of performance required are typically determined by you, your student, the certifying agency, and the dive environment and activities. When you begin teaching scuba to students with special needs, you may find yourself reevaluating some of the skills you teach or the way you teach them. Keep in mind that safety is still the primary concern, and should never be sacrificed for comfort or convenience. At the same time, it can benefit you and all of your students if you periodically question your own teaching. Analyze each of the skills you teach to see if they are really necessary for the safety of the diver. Also analyze each component of the skill to see if it is really necessary for safe, proper performance or if it has just somehow become a part of the process.

Fortunately, many of the skills you teach and the manner in which you teach them will be effective with all of your students. However, for some skills or with some students, you will find it necessary to modify your techniques or even start from scratch. When this is the case, be patient and creative and use plenty of common sense. Also, allow your students to experiment and be prepared to learn from them. It may also be necessary to alter the amount of time you have your students spend working on certain skills. For example, a student who doesn't use fins will not need to spend time working on kick techniques. At the same time, because this student can't use fins to assist in buoyancy control, he may need to spend extra time working on buoyancy control through the use of his BC and breathing techniques.

REVIEW OF MAIN POINTS

- When teaching scuba skills, focus on safety and proper performance rather than style.
- When teaching scuba skills, be creative and open to suggestion, without compromising safety.
- Evaluate each skill, as well as the components of the skill, to determine if it is necessary for safety while scuba diving.
- Teach the student to recognize circumstances which call for assistance from a buddy to accomplish the task as quickly as possible.
- Acting as a buddy for a diver with special needs may call for a level of buddy support which is higher than usually practiced. It is important that the diver and his buddy be fully aware of each other's abilities and limitations, as well as the level of support which will be necessary during the dive. It is equally important that all divers satisfy themselves that their dive buddies are capable of providing the necessary support.
- A diver who is unable to manipulate her BC controls or weight system must always be able to establish positive buoyancy through body movements or breathing techniques.
- A diver who is not capable of acting independently in the water must never be left alone in the water.
- A diver with special needs must accept full responsibility for his own safety including supervising his equipment, participating in dive planning and evaluating the knowledge and skills of his dive buddies.

APPLYING YOUR KNOWLEDGE

1. Analyze the scuba skills you teach in your program and identify which skills are truly necessary for safety while scuba diving.

2. Analyze the techniques you teach for performing the necessary skills and determine which components of the skill are truly necessary for safe performance.

3. In your own words, describe style versus technique, and identify criteria for safe technique while performing scuba skills.

4. Identify and describe situations in which a diver with special needs might be encouraged to ask for assistance even though he is capable of performing the skill unassisted.

5. Identify areas of concern regarding safety and equipment during performance of various scuba skills.

6. Describe techniques for performing various scuba skills.

7. Outline plans for assisting divers with special needs to enter and exit the water at appropriate local dive sites. Identify any potential dangers present in the plans and what safeguards must be put into place. Also identify the level of staff support necessary to conduct safe, efficient entries and exits.

8. Discuss potential differences in the level of buddy support necessary when acting as a buddy for divers with various levels of ability. Identify and discuss special concerns you may have when acting as a buddy for a diver who is unable to act independently while diving.

REFERENCES

Emmerson, L., Ravendale, J., Atterbury, S., Isabelle, H., North York Y-Nauts, Toronto Snorkelauts, Carmichael, B., Garrett, G., & Murray, R.. (n.d.). Skin diving for the physically handicapped. (Available from Moray Wheels Adaptive Scuba Association, PO Box 1660 GMF, Boston, MA. 02205)

Green, J. S., & Miles B. H. (1987).Use of mask, fins, snorkel, and scuba equipment in aquatics for the disabled. Palaestra, 3(4), 12-17.

National Oceanic and Atmospheric Administration (1991). Diving with disabilities. In NOAA diving manual diving for science and technology (pp. A1-A11). Silver Spring, MD: National Oceanic and Atmospheric Administration.

Open Waters (1994). Open waters scuba diving for everyone: A guide to making diving training accessible to people with disabilities. (Available from Open Waters c/o Alpha One, 127 Main St., South Portland, ME 04106)

Petrofsky, J. S. (1994). Diving with spinal cord injury. Palaestra, 11(1), 30-31, 49-51.

Robinson, J., & Fox, A. D. (1987). Scuba diving with disabilities. Champaign, IL: Leisure Press.

Waring, W. (1984). Concerns for diving in the spinal cord injury population. Paper presented at the national conference of the Council for National Cooperation in Aquatics, Fort Worth , TX.

YMCA of the USA (1987). Aquatics for special populations. Champaign, IL: Human Kinetics.

Chapter 5

Wheelchairs

CHAPTER OVERVIEW

To many of us, a wheelchair is only that, a chair with wheels. However, to someone who uses a wheelchair for his activities of daily living, the wheelchair may be more than a rolling chair. It is a part of himself.

Knowing this, it should come as no surprise that a great deal of thought and care goes into selecting a wheelchair. In the March/April 1993 issue of Sports 'N Spokes Magazine, Peter Axelson of Beneficial Designs Inc., identified 22 manufacturers of wheelchairs and 38 factors to consider when selecting a chair. Factors that must be considered when evaluating wheelchairs include functional aspects such as weight, material and dimensions, as well as color and upholstery, warranty, delivery and cost. While some chairs can be purchased stock from the manufacturer, others are custom made, and the cost can be in the thousands of dollars.

As an instructor working with students with disabilities, you will not need detailed technical knowledge of wheelchairs. However, a working knowledge of wheelchairs and how to handle them will improve your level of comfort and enable you better to assist your students should they request it. Remember that wheelchairs are both personal and expensive. There is no need to be apprehensive when dealing with them, but you should handle them with care and respect.

In this section you will find information regarding the parts and features of a wheelchair, as well as some basic tips on handling wheelchairs. You will also find basic information on techniques for assisting someone out of or into a wheelchair. **Remember always to use proper lifting techniques and to be careful, as there is some risk of injury to both you and the person you are assisting.**

PARTS AND FEATURES OF WHEELCHAIRS

In order to discuss the various parts and features of a wheelchair, you must be familiar with some of the different models of chairs.

Traditional Model

This model of wheelchair is the one most of picture when we think of wheelchairs and is typically found in health care institutions or large facilities such as airports. Generally, these chairs are designed for comfort and stability, and are used by individuals who may require assistance in propelling their chairs. This type of chair may be referred to variously as a "standard", "hospital"or "medical" model chair.

Features

- Push handles at the top of and protruding to the rear of the seat back.
- Brakes for locking the wheels.
- Footrests, also referred to as footplates, pedestals, or platforms. The footrests may be attached, and therefore removed, in a variety of ways. Ask the person using the chair how the footrests are attached.
- Removable armrests.
- Large rear wheels referred to as the main wheels.
- Small forward wheels referred to as casters.
- Tipping lever which protrudes to the rear of the chair at the bottom of the frame. This lever can be used by the person pushing the chair to tip it backwards when negotiating barriers such as curbs.
- The traditional model chair typically can be collapsed or folded to make it more compact.

Maneuvering the Chair

- Ask the person using the chair how she prefers to proceed.
- Never move or maneuver an occupied chair without communicating with the occupant to ensure that he or she is prepared.
- Avoid abrupt changes in direction or speed.
- Make sure that all body parts are inside the chair. Body parts which protrude can get caught in the wheels or bang against or get caught on obstacles.
- Pay particular attention to the person's feet, and make sure that they don't fall off of the footrests. This condition, sometimes known as "foot fall" can go undetected by individuals who lack sensation, and can cause serious injury. Pay particular attention when the individual using the chair is prone to spasms.
- When crossing rough ground, tilt the chair back on the main wheels into a "wheelie" position. Otherwise the front casters can get hung up on rocks, sticks, etc.
- When descending steep slopes or curbs, face uphill or away from the curb and position the chair so the occupant is also facing up the hill or away from the curb. Walk backwards, controlling the chair as you descend.
- When ascending a curb, face the curb and position the chair so the occupant is also facing the curb. Tip the chair back towards you and push it as close to the curb as possible, so the casters are beyond the curb. Lower the casters to the higher surface, lift and push the chair up onto the curb. You may find it helpful to push one leg or hip into the back of the chair.
- When going up stairs, turn your back to the stairs and position the chair so that the occupant also has his back towards the stairs. Tip the chair back towards yourself and back up the stairs, rolling the chair on the main wheels.
- When going down stairs, face down the steps and position the chair so that the occupant also faces down the stairs. Tip the chair back towards yourself and walk forward down the stairs.

Manipulating the Chair

- Open the chair by pushing down on the outer edges of the sides of the seat.
- Collapse the chair using the following procedure:
  1. Stand to either side of the chair, facing the main wheel.
  2. Grasp the front and back edges of the seat, placing your hands on the centerline of the seat.
  3. Pull up on the seat.
- Pick up the chair by holding the frame.
- Do not pick up the chair by the armrests, as they may pull out.
- Be careful about picking up the chair by the wheels, as the chair may rotate.

Everyday and Sport Chairs

These chairs are light-weight, maneuverable, and easy to push and accelerate. Typically, these chairs are used by individuals who are capable of pushing themselves and by wheelchair athletes.

Features

- Typically, these chairs don't have armrests, push handles or footplates.
- The feet are placed on a solid bar at the lower front end of the frame. A roll bar, which prevents the foot bar from gouging the floor may be found just below and behind the foot bar.
- These chairs may also have anti-tip casters in back, to prevent the chair from tipping over backwards. Anti-tip casters may have to be removed for maneuvers, such as going up or down stairs, which require tipping the chair back at an angle.
- These chairs may or may not have brakes.
- The frames on these chairs are typically solid and do not fold. However, the chair back may fold down onto the seat for easier storage.
- The wheels on these chairs are typically easy to remove using a quick-release mechanism.

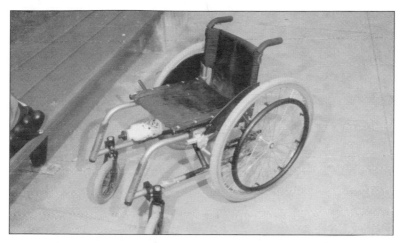

FIGURE 5-1

FIGURE 5-2

- Wheels on these chairs may be at an angle, referred to as camber. This increased camber provides more stability for the chair.
- Adjustable axles allow for different wheel placement.

Figure 5-1 shows an everyday model chair with a variety of features, including push handles, brakes, and quick release wheels.

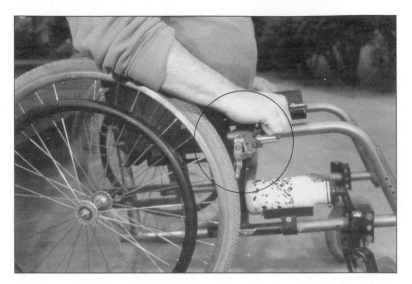

FIGURE 5-3

FIGURE 5-4

In figure 5-2 the brake is disengaged, while in figure 5-3 the brake is on. Notice the quick release wheels (figure 5-4).

This chair does fold, becoming very compact when the wheels are removed and the chair is collapsed for storage (figure 5-5).

FIGURE 5-5

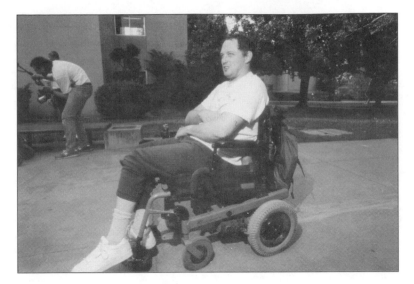

FIGURE 5-6

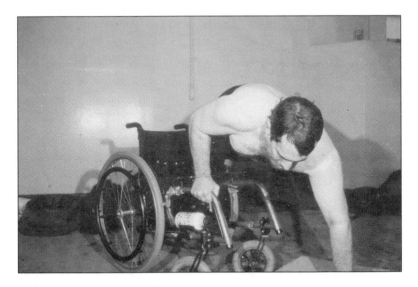

FIGURE 5-7

Manipulating Everyday and Sport Chairs

* Become familiar with removal and replacement of the wheels. You should be able to do this quickly and easily.
* Become familiar with the preferred axle position of the person using the chair.
* Be careful when picking the chair up by the wheels as you may unintentionally release them.

Motorized or Power Chairs

These chairs are self propelled and usually powered by an automotive battery. Typically, these chairs are extremely heavy and can't be collapsed with the battery in place. While these chairs are not very portable themselves, they do provide a great deal of independence for the user. Notice the heavy frame of the Motorized chair shown in figure 5-6. Frequently, individuals using these chairs will drive a vehicle equipped with a lift for hoisting the chair into the vehicle.

TRANSFERS

Transfers is a catch all term applied to techniques used to move from one position to another, by individuals with impaired mobility. The ability to transfer safely out of, or into, a wheelchair is important for individuals who use wheelchairs. Many of your students will be able to do this unassisted, in which case, it is best to stand by and assist only if it becomes necessary. However, for those students who may require assistance, there are some basic safety considerations and techniques of which you should be aware.

Safety Considerations

* Always ask the person requesting assistance if they have a preferred method or suggestions for accomplishing the transfer. Remember, they have done this before. When possible allow the person being transferred to be in charge of the transfer.

- Handle the person firmly but slowly and gently. In many cases this person may be using a wheelchair due to an injury which occurred as a result of falling or being dropped. It is important that the person feel as secure as possible during the transfer.
- When more than one assistant is available, the stronger person should typically be positioned at the upper body of the person being transferred.
- Whenever possible, the person being transferred should see the area or object to which she is being transferred.
- Always be aware of your own safety as well as that of the person you are assisting.
- Minimize the distance of the transfer by placing the chair as close as possible to the transfer point.
- Make sure the chair is as stable as possible by securing the brakes and pointing the casters straight ahead.
- Remove any objects from the chair which may interfere with the transfer. Objects which must be removed may include parts of the chair itself such as armrests or foot pedestals.
- Make sure that you have secure footing.

FIGURE 5-8

FIGURE 5-9

FIGURE 5-10

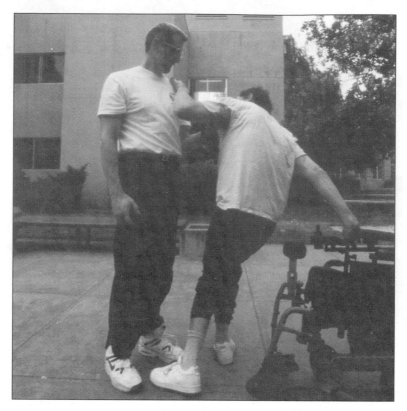

FIGURE 5-11

- Stand as close as possible to the person, and position yourself so you can use proper lifting techniques such as lifting with your legs and not your back. Keep your back straight.
- Position your feet far enough apart to maintain your balance. You may find that placing one foot forward of the other allows you to shift position or move more easily.
- It is easier to transfer between objects of the same height. A board referred to as a "transfer board" or a "sliding board" can be used to bridge the gap between the objects. Make sure the board is securely anchored at both ends.
- If the person being transferred has more strength or mobility on one side of their body, position them so that

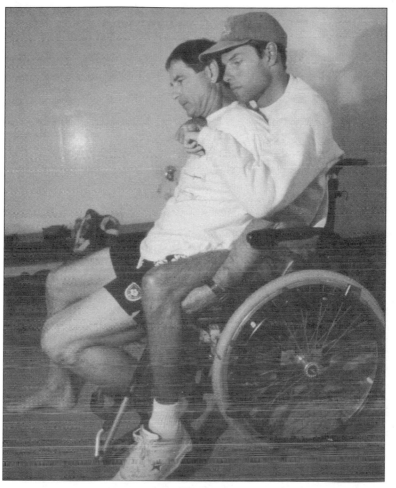

FIGURE 5 13

they can use that side. Be prepared to assist from the
weaker side.

- To perform a one-person assist, it is recommended that
  the person being assisted have enough strength to lift her
  body weight off of the surface on which she is sitting.

FIGURE 5-13

Assisting an Individual Capable of Self Help

In come cases the individual does not require a great deal of
assistance. Figures 5-8, 5-9, 5-10, and 5-11 illustrate one
technique for assisting these individuals. In figure 5-8, notice
how the individual in the chair has moved forward to the
front edge of the chair. Also notice how the assistant is
braced to provide support, and has placed his feet to block
the individuals feet and prevent them from sliding. In figures
5-9 and 5-10 the assistant provides support as necessary
while continuing to block the feet. In figure 5-11, the individ-

ual is preparing to move away from the assistant. It is important that the assistant continue to block the individual's feet and provide support until the individual states clearly that it is no longer necessary.

Single Assistant Lifts

In those instances where only a single assistant is present, there are a number of techniques for transferring into and out of a wheelchair. Figures 5-12 and 5-13 illustrate two such methods. When attempting any transfer such as that in figure 5-12, it is vital that the brakes on the chair be engaged. While these techniques can be quick and convenient, they can also pose considerable risk for both the individual and the assistant. These techniques require strength on the part of the assistant and a lot of trust on the part of the individual being lifted. Remember that after a dive the assistant may be cold and tired. Also, when wearing wetsuits and gloves mobility and dexterity are impaired. When considering attempting such lifts, be objective about your abilities. Just because you did it successfully this morning does not mean you can do it safely after the third dive of the day.

Stand and Pivot Transfer

This transfer is used when the individual being transferred is capable of very little self help, and only one assistant is available. It might also be necessary when transferring in a confined space such as a bathroom stall. When performing this transfer, use the following procedure:

- The student should be sitting on the front edge of the chair with the feet on the floor.
- Stand facing the student and position your hands under the students buttocks.
- Control the student's legs and feet by placing them between your legs and feet.
- If the student has adequate strength and control, she may use her arms to hold on to you. Otherwise, it may be necessary to control her arms by placing them between your body and the her body.

- Have the student place her chin over your shoulder. This will provide control for her head while allowing her to observe the transfer point.
- Tilt the student's torso forward toward you and lift her clear of the chair seat.
- Pivot the student while controlling her legs and feet with your legs and feet. Be prepared for the knees to buckle and prevent this by using your legs as braces or supports.
- Lower the student to the transfer point.
- Once the student is sitting on the transfer object, continue to assist in controlling her torso by sliding your hands to her back, while leaving her chin on your shoulder. This will prevent the student from falling either forward or backwards. Do not release the student until you are sure that her arms are in position to support her or she is secured in some other manner. This is extremely important for students having little or no control of their torso.

Sitting Transfer with One Assistant

This transfer requires that the student have enough strength and dexterity to control his upper body, extend his arms, and support the weight of his upper body on his arms. It requires only one assistant. When performing this transfer, use the following procedure:

- Position the chair at about a 45° angle as close as possible to the transfer object.
- Extend the student's legs and place them on the transfer object.
- Position your hands under the student's buttocks or around their waist.
- As you lift, the student should simultaneously press up out of the seat of the chair by extending her arms, pushing against the armrests of the chair. Lift until the student is clear of the chair seat.
- With the feet as a pivot point, swing the student into position on the transfer point.
- Do not release the student until she is in a secure position and will not fall.

Sitting Transfer with Two Assistants

This transfer might be used when the individual in the chair is capable of very little self help and two assistants are available. When performing this transfer use the following procedure:

- Position the chair at about a 45° angle, as close as possible to the transfer object.
- Have the student cross his forearms over his chest.
- Position one assistant behind the student, facing the student's back.
- Position the other assistant beside the legs of the student.
- The assistant behind the student should reach underneath the student's armpits and grip the student's forearms or have the student grip his forearms.
- While lifting the student, the assistant behind the student should press the student's forearms gently but firmly in against the chest and then lift. Do not lift up on the armpits, as this can cause injury to the shoulder joints or spine.
- The assistant at the legs should cradle the legs with one arm under the upper legs and one arm under the lower legs.
- Both assistants should lift simultaneously and transfer the student to the transfer point or object.
- The assistant at the student's back should not release the student until the student is in a secure position and will not fall.

Side Transfer with Two Assistants

This transfer might be used when two assistants are available to help the individual transfer. When performing this transfer, use the following procedure:

- The assistants should position themselves on either side of the chair, facing the individual.
- The arms of the person to be transferred should be draped over the shoulders of the assistants. The assistants should reach around behind the individual and get a good grip on each other's hand or forearm.

- Each assistant should place one arm underneath the knee or upper leg of the person to be transferred. Again the assistants should get a good grip on the other's hand or forearm.
- Using proper lifting techniques lift the person out of the chair.

CHAPTER SUMMARY

Wheelchairs may be a fact of everyday life for some of your students or staff members. As an instructor working with these individuals, you should be comfortable handling wheelchairs. You should also be comfortable and competent in assisting someone to transfer out of or into a wheelchair. As always, a willingness to accept suggestions and some common sense will usually get the job done.

Keep in mind that during transfers, there is some risk to you and the person you are assisting. It is important that you become familiar with basic wheelchair and transfer techniques, so you will be able to assist your students safely and effectively.

REVIEW OF MAIN POINTS

- A person who uses a wheelchair in his daily life may consider the chair to be a part of himself.
- Handle chairs with care and respect.
- Traditional model wheelchairs are generally used by individuals who may require assistance in propelling their chairs.
- Typically, the armrests and foot pedestals on Traditional Model Chairs are removable.
- Do not attempt to pick up Traditional Model Wheelchairs by the armrests as they may pull out.
- Typically, Traditional Model Wheelchairs can be collapsed for ease of storage.
- When assisting someone who uses a wheelchair, ask her if she has a preferred technique or method.
- Be careful when picking up a chair by the wheels as the chair may rotate.

- Everyday or Sport Wheelchairs are generally used by individuals who can propel their chair without assistance.
- The main wheels on Everyday or Sport Chairs are easily removed.
- Motorized or Power Wheelchairs are typically used by individuals with more extreme disabilities.
- When assisting someone during transfers, ask them if they have a preferred method.
- When assisting someone to transfer, be firm but gentle.
- Always be aware of the safety of both yourself and the person you are assisting.
- Minimize the distance over which the transfer must take place.
- Always use proper lifting techniques, keeping your back straight and making sure that you are in a good position to lift the weight.
- To perform a one-person assist, the person being transferred should have enough strength to press himself off of the surface on which he is sitting.
- Do not release the person you are assisting until they are in a secure position and will not fall.
- When lifting someone from behind, do not pull up on her armpits as this may cause injury to the shoulders or spine. Instead, press her forearms gently but firmly against her chest as you lift.

APPLYING YOUR KNOWLEDGE

1. Identify three general models or categories of wheelchairs and describe the typical user of each model.
2. Describe foot fall as it applies to a person using a wheelchair, explain why it is cause for concern.
3. Describe techniques for assisting a person using a wheelchair to ascend or descend steep slopes, curbs or stairs.
4. Discuss what is meant by the term transfer, and discuss general safety considerations when performing transfers.
5. Identify three types of transfers and explain how each should be performed.

REFERENCES

Axelson, P. (1993). Wheelchair comparison. Sports 'N Spokes, 18 (6), 34-57.

Lasko-McCarthey, P., & Knopf, K. G. (1992). Adapted physical education for adults with disabilities. Dubuque, IA: Eddie Bowers Publishing, Inc.

Miller, P. D. (ed.). (1995). Fitness programming and physical disability. Champaign, IL:Human Kinetics.

Sherrill C. (1993). Adapted physical activity, recreation and sport: Crossdisciplinary and lifespan (4th ed.). WCB Brown & Benchmark: Dubuque.

Chapter 6

Facilities

CHAPTER OVERVIEW

In July of 1990 the Americans With Disabilities Act, typically referred to as the ADA, became law. One purpose of this act is to ensure that persons with disabilities enjoy full access to and enjoyment of public facilities, including swimming pools. As explained by Dr. Alison Osinski, the law intends that "Individuals with disabilities must be able to enter, use, and exit a pool with little or no assistance, and without drawing undue or unwanted attention to themselves." Unfortunately, for most of us this will not be the reality of the training facilities we use.

FACILITIES EVALUATION

When evaluating a facility for use in your program, you must consider the building itself as well as the swimming pool, locker rooms, classroom, and parking. Remember that while an ideal facility would be nice, it is not a necessity. With a little creativity, less than ideal facilities will do just fine.

This section of the guide will discuss how to evaluate potential training facilities. Without going into great architectural detail, practical considerations will be presented for determining the suitability of a facility. Also, where possible, I will offer practical suggestions for adapting the facility to accommodate the needs of your students. Keep in mind that perhaps the best way to evaluate a facility and plan necessary accommodations is to get in a wheelchair and go to that facility at the normal class time. Explore the areas you will typically be using and see what works and what doesn't. It is also a good idea to enlist someone who uses a wheel chair as part of her daily life to assist you in the facility evaluation.

Please keep in mind that the following lists represent a practical look at the bare minimums that help to make a facility accessible or appropriate for scuba programs for divers with disabilities. More detailed information is available in the text _Aquatics for Special Populations_ by the YMCA. Information on the ADA and swimming pool modification is also available in an excellent article by Dr. Alison Osinski entitled _Modifying Public Swimming Pools to Comply with the Americans with Disabilities Act_. The article was published in the summer 1993 issue of _Palaestra_.

The Building
Items to be Evaluated

* There should be plenty of accessible parking.
* Walkways and entryways should be firm, smooth, and at least 48" wide.
* Walkways and entryways should be well lighted.
* Entryways or doorways should be at least 32" wide, with a threshold no higher than 1/2".
* Doors should be easy to open and should close slowly. Ideally, doors should open under their own power or have lever type handles. Buildings with revolving doors or turnstiles should have alternate entryways.
* Floors should be slip resistant and hallways should be at least 48" wide.
* There should be accessible toilet facilities.
* At least one drinking fountain should be accessible to persons who use wheelchairs. The fountain should be operated by a push bar or lever, not by a knob or button.
* At least one telephone should be accessible to persons who use a wheelchair.
* Buildings with more than one level should have elevators.
* Ramps should be installed where necessary to avoid stairs.
* Locker rooms, classrooms, and the pool should be on the same level.

Suggestions for Accommodation

- One very important step is to be sure that alternate entry-ways are clearly marked and easily found. Also, it is important to check the lighting of these areas. Frequently, scuba classes are held at night and an unlighted area can present hazards to anybody. If the alternate entry areas are remote and/or dark, make sure that no one uses them alone. Keep in mind however, that alternate entryways may require moving gear over greater distances. On the other hand they may put you closer to where you want to be. It may even be a good idea to designate that entry as the one to be used by the entire class. Use common sense and enlist the cooperation of all class members as well as the staff who operate the building.

- If some of your students have impaired mobility, and there are no elevators available, try to use facilities on the first floor. This may mean that instead of the regular classroom you will be around a table in the lobby or at the side of the pool. Use common sense when comparing the possible distractions in this setting versus the logistics of having your students climb steps. Also keep in mind that access to rest room facilities is important.

- If stairways, rough ground, or difficult doors are an issue, it is helpful to have staff members available in the parking lot or at the entryway to assist students as necessary. Depending on the size of the staff, this may not be possible if students are late, so stress the importance of being on time. Also remember that strips of carpet, plastic fencing, or wood can provide firm clean walkways.

Locker Rooms
Items to be Evaluated

The locker room should be connected to the swimming pool area and have the following:

- changing tables
- private stalls for changing
- accessible toilets with handrails
- chairs or benches with handrails for sitting in the showers
- hand held shower heads

Suggestions for Accommodation

- Temporary stalls can be erected for privacy, using partitions, curtains, or even tents.
- Hand held showers can be installed.
- Plastic chairs such as those used for patio or beach furniture can be used for shower chairs.
- Temporary changing tables can be made by placing pads on the floor or on benches pushed together. Make sure that any benches used are wide enough and stable enough to support the person.
- Tape insulation over exposed hot water pipes.

The Pool
Items to be Evaluated

- The water temperature should be at least 80° Fahrenheit, and the air temperature should be within 3-5° F of the water temp.
- The pool deck should be slip resistant, but matting, grids, etc. should not impede the mobility of persons who use wheelchairs, crutches or canes.
- The pool decks should be uncluttered with a minimum of 8 feet on all sides of the pool.
- The pool deck should be at the same level as the surface of the water.
- The pool should have both shallow and deep sections, but there should not be any sudden changes in depth.
- The pool lights should not give off any heat.
- Wide gutters or skimmer pots should be covered.
- Outdoor pools should have shaded areas.
- Swimmers should be able to enter the pool via any of the following: ramps, wide shallow steps with rails, stairs with rails, lifts or hoists which utilize a chair or sling, transfer tiers to make it easy to move out of a wheelchair into the water, or plastic pool chairs which can be wheeled into the water. The depth of water in the entry area should be shallow so that swimmers who are able can enter and stand unassisted.

Suggestions for Accommodation

- Strips of carpet or plastic runners used to protect carpeting can provide covering for rough pool decks. Make sure that in covering the rough stuff, you don't create a slippery surface which can be dangerous.
- Crutches, canes, walkers, or other assistive devices should have slip resistant tips on the end, and those tips should be in good condition.
- Pads can be placed on the pool deck to provide a comfortable and safe place for students to sit or lie while working with gear or entering or exiting the water.
- Students can wear exposure suits while in the water. Aside from providing warmth, this will simulate open water diving conditions. It will also protect the students from abrasions due to rough surface.
- Students can bring robes or jackets to wear when moving between the pool and the locker room.
- Areas can be designated for staging of equipment while other areas are designated to remain clear and uncluttered at all times. This will make it easier for everybody to move around.
- When necessary, students can be carried into the water using plastic chairs, stretchers, backboards, etc. This should be determined in cooperation with the student. Be aware of the potential for injury to the student as well as for those who are carrying the student into the water. Make sure that the carrying device is appropriate and adequate support is available for the carriers.
- Flotation devices typical of scuba training, such as surf mats or floats, can be used instead of railings for support in the water.
- In some cases, shields can be installed between pool lights and the students. However, this can be tricky, as obstructing the lights can create safety hazards.
- When using outdoor pools, temporary shelters such as awnings or tents can be erected to protect students from the environment.

The Classroom
Items to be evaluated
- The classroom should be wheelchair-accessible and well lighted. Avoid classrooms with tight corners, clutter, or steps, as these make it difficult for individuals who use wheelchairs or other assistive devices.
- The classroom should have tables or desks suitable for use by individuals who use wheelchairs.
- Tape recorders or other audiovisual equipment should be available for students who have difficulty writing.

Suggestions for Accommodation
- The use of videos, posters, and bulletin boards can make things much easier for the class.
- For those students who have difficulty writing, you can ask for volunteer notetakers. Make sure their handwriting is legible.
- Handouts minimize the need for notetaking and can clarify your lecture or comments. The minimum print size for handouts for students with visual impairments is 14-point, and 16 point is preferred.
- You may also wish to tape your lectures and make those tapes available to your students.
- In some cases, it would be nice to have available materials in Braille or closed caption. Unfortunately, scuba materials produced using these techniques are rare.
- Remember, for those students with impaired hearing, vision, or speaking abilities, proper communication techniques are extremely important. Always try to:
  1. Place yourself in good light.
  2. Face the student to whom you are speaking.
  3. Speak slowly and distinctly, without gum, candy or other objects in your mouth.
  4. Use written communication or interpreters when necessary.
  5. Ask questions that can be answered with short simple answers.
  6. Make sure that the appropriate information has been understood.

CHAPTER SUMMARY

Facilities which have been designed or retrofitted with persons with disabilities in mind can be a great asset to your program. Such facilities enhance access and comfort and minimize inconvenience for you and your class. Unfortunately such facilities are few and far between. To locate such facilities, you should check with local hospitals, recreation programs, and programs offering rehabilitation or therapy.

Fortunately, ideal facilities are not a necessity for a successful scuba program. With patience, advance planning and a little creativity you can make even a fortress suit your needs. Work with your students or staff members who use wheelchairs to identify suitable facilities or to modify existing sites to make them suitable. A facility which is less than ideal is better than no facility at all. Ultimately, the main concern is the safety of your students and the quality of their learning experience.

REVIEW OF MAIN POINTS

• When evaluating a facility for use in a scuba program for divers with special needs, consider the building, parking, locker rooms, classrooms, and the pool itself.

• Pay particular attention to any conditions which can create a hazard for your students. Don't create new hazards in your efforts to improve comfort or access. For example, in attempting to protect students from being burned by pool lights, don't obstruct the lights. This can create safety hazards as well as make instruction and learning more difficult

• When using outdoor pools, protect your students from the environment.

• Always use good communication techniques, especially with students who have impaired vision, hearing, or speech.

APPLYING YOUR KNOWLEDGE

1. Identify items which should be evaluated for each of the following components of the training facility: the building, locker rooms, the pool, and classrooms.

2. For each item identified above, provide a description of desirable characteristics as well as suggestions for modifications to accommodate persons with disabilities.

REFERENCES

Open Waters (1994). Open waters scuba diving for everyone: A guide to making diving training accessible to people with disabilities. (Available from Open Waters c/o Alpha One, 127 Main St., South Portland, ME 04106)

Osinski, A. (1993). Modifying public swimming pools to comply with provisions of the americans with disabilities act. Palaestra, 9(4), 13-18.

YMCA of the USA (1987). Aquatics for Special Populations. Champaign, IL: Human Kinetics.

Chapter 7

Developing Your Program

CHAPTER OVERVIEW

When developing a scuba program involving divers with special needs, one of the first questions to ask yourself is "will I limit the program strictly to divers with special needs?" Jill Robinson, co-author of Diving with Disabilities feels that scuba instructors should offer "equal opportunity courses." Dorothy Shrout, co-founder of NIADD, also advocates classes which are open to everyone. In fact, Dorothy has said that one of the most enjoyable aspects of having divers with disabilities in a class is watching the barriers and discomfort disappear as the class comes together. I also prefer teaching classes open to all divers. Ultimately however, this is a personal choice based on your own teaching philosophy, the needs of your students, and the staff available to support you.

Once you have decided whom you would like to see participate in your program, you must consider a number of other things. Obviously, you must find students for your classes, so you may be recruiting outside the areas where you typically look for students. Also, you must plan and develop course schedules and activities that are appropriate for the members of the class. That means you must develop the knowledge and skills necessary to provide safe, effective and enjoyable instruction.

In this section, we will discuss some of the resources available to assist you in finding students and developing the skills and knowledge necessary to implement your program. These resources include professionals in areas such as rehabilitation and recreation, as well as people and organizations active in adapted scuba. We will also discuss some of the considerations for scheduling a class and selecting open water training sites.

FINDING STUDENTS

Many of you may be interested in teaching scuba to persons with special needs because you know or have been approached by such an individual. Others of you may be motivated by a desire to share scuba with people who otherwise might not get to experience the underwater world. Regardless of what got you started, you must have students enrolled in your program, and this means promoting your classes. Just like any customers, many students with special needs will become aware of your program through the normal means such as word of mouth, or through the local dive center or recreation department.

Unfortunately, many potential scuba divers will not believe or even be aware, that scuba is an option for them.

There are a number of resources you can utilize to get the message to these individuals, some of which are identified in a list at the end of this section. Keep in mind that just like any scuba program, a program which involves divers with special needs may take a while to get going. Be patient and use the creativity that all instructors need to be successful. Generally, you will find yourself doing and saying the same things as always. The difference is that you will be saying them in new environments and to new groups of potential students. You will also find that while individuals with disabilities may have some concerns specific to their needs or disabilities, many of their concerns are the same as any other students.

As you move outside the traditional scuba community, you will encounter and work with professionals in fields such as physical therapy or adapted physical education. While most of us have heard these terms, we may not have given much thought to just what it is these people do. However, it is important that we understand the goals and objectives of these professionals. Accordingly, at the end of this section, you will find a list of practical descriptions of some concepts and professions related to adapted scuba. Don't forget that many of the professionals you meet will not know anything about scuba and the benefits it offers to all divers. They may even resist your efforts to involve their clients in scuba training. However, this is a great opportunity to educate them, recruit them as new students, and enlist them to help promote your program.

Also keep in mind that when first working with divers with disabilities, it will be a learning experience for both of you. Jill Robinson, co-author of Diving with Disabilities, advises that, when starting out, you should not rush out and recruit large numbers of students. In my experience, starting out working with one or two students with special needs will allow you to develop a good level of comfort. Eventually, you will get a good feel for the number of students you can comfortably work with at one time. Properly trained assistants are a big help here.

ACTIVE ADAPTED SCUBA GROUPS

For an instructor developing a program offering scuba to persons with physical disabilities or special needs, it is always helpful to know what resources are available. Fortunately, diving for individuals with disabilities is receiving more and more attention these days, so the list of people and organizations active in this area is growing. Unfortunately, this means that providing a truly comprehensive list of resources is extremely unlikely. However, the organizations listed at the end of this section will give you a good start in becoming familiar with who is active in scuba for divers with special needs.

STAFF-TO-STUDENT RATIOS

Many experts recommend that the first session be conducted in a one-on-one situation between you and the student. Such a session will allow you to become familiar with the student, assess the student's needs and determine what accommodations may be necessary for her safety and comfort. This session is also an opportunity for you to evaluate the student's confidence and comfort in the water, as well as her ability to handle the equipment. You may also want to use this time to demonstrate emergency procedures.

Some experienced instructors stress that scuba instruction for persons with disabilities requires familiarity with the rehabilitation process, strong instructor skills, and constant attention to safety. The British Sports Association for the Disabled goes so far as to say that individuals with severe disabilities should receive their initial training in special courses supervised by doctors.

The necessity for one-on-one training or medical supervision may best be determined after an evaluation of the abilities of the student in question. It is important not to stereotype any group of people. Just because someone is said to "have a physical disability" does not mean that they are ill or "disabled." Many individuals with disabilities maintain high levels of both physical fitness and health. They may be outstanding swimmers and possess high levels of comfort, strength and stamina in the water. It is very likely that such individuals will not require any special instruction and will not have any problem keeping up with the rest of the class.

However, as with any scuba class, it is important to have an adequate number of appropriately trained staff members. The number of staff required will be determined by the size of the class, the extent of any special needs that the students may have, your own personal standards, and the policies or standards of the agency through which you certify your students.

STAFF TRAINING

A question often asked is "What specialized training should staff members have in order to work with divers with special needs?" This question addresses an important issue, and can spark considerable debate. As when teaching any scuba class, you should have enough staff members with appropriate training in scuba skills and knowledge. Furthermore, it may be appropriate to have personnel on site with training in medicine, physical therapy, recreation or similar professions. Your staffing needs may vary with your students and if you are unsure as to what is appropriate, you should discuss the situation with the student and any health care professionals working with the student.

It has been my experience that as long as the staff members have adequate scuba background and are honest, open, and receptive to the students, the job will get done. You should also be aware that training for divers wishing to act as dive buddies or companions for divers with special needs is available through the various clubs and training agencies active in adapted scuba. It may also be beneficial for you and your staff to volunteer at local rehabilitation centers or hospitals. This can provide invaluable experience working with individuals with physical disabilities.

It is also a good idea to enlist divers with disabilities to assist you in teaching your classes. These individuals will serve as role models for your students. They may also be in a better position than you to anticipate accommodations which will prevent or remove barriers and ease the learning process for your students.

It is also helpful to be aware of other situations which may be more likely to arise when working with divers with special needs. For example, you may be approached by a buddy team consisting of an individual with a disability and a friend. In this situation, if the individual has a severe disability, it may be advisable for the friend to participate in scuba training prior to the training of the person with the disability. This can facilitate the training of the companion and provide a valuable assistant for the instructor when the other member of the dive team begins instruction. On the other hand, you don't want to deprive the students of the enjoyment of taking the class together. This is a situation where adequate staffing can make a big difference in how many students you accept into the class, as well as in how you conduct the class.

Always keep in mind that you must evaluate the companion just as carefully as any other student. It is possible that the companion is not really interested in diving, but is there simply because of the other person's desire to scuba dive. In this case, the companion may not be of much assistance to the instructor. In fact, it is possible that the able-bodied companion will have more difficulty learning to dive than the student with the disability. Remember, just because someone is said to "have a disability", does not mean they are "disabled." It is just as true that just because someone is said to be "able-bodied", does not mean that they are physically or mentally prepared to learn and perform the required scuba skills. Many times I have been surprised by what students could and couldn't do, or would and wouldn't do.

When teaching classes which consist of both students with disabilities and students without disabilities, it is important to encourage cooperation between all students. Furthermore, as with any class you teach, you must be aware of how staff time is allocated. For example, if one student requires a great deal of time and attention, it is easy for you to concentrate on that individual, allowing the rest of the class to be taught by assistants. Conversely, you may have an assistant work closely with one student while you focus on the rest of the class.

Either situation can result in some students feeling that they are not receiving enough of your time, while others may feel that they are unfairly singled out for special attention. Eventually, this can cause misunderstanding and resentment. Probably all of us have encountered such situations while teaching scuba, but in classes which integrate divers with and without special needs, the issue may be more sensitive. Once again, adequate staff with appropriate training can prevent or at least minimize such problems.

THE "MOTHER HEN" SYNDROME

When first teaching students with special needs, even experienced instructors may be overly concerned and have a tendency to demonstrate what I call the "Mother Hen" Syndrome. These instructors constantly fuss over their students, like a mother hen over her chicks. Typically, the instructor is concerned about the safety or enjoyment of the student and simply wants to protect him from harm or embarrassment. Unfortunately, regardless of the motivation, such over-protectiveness is an obstacle to quality instruction.

Many individuals with disabilities have worked hard to establish their independence in daily life and they have been successful at doing so. These individuals may find it irritating, offensive or even demeaning to have an instructor fuss over them as if they are helpless, and they are justified in feeling that way. Even if they understand and accept the motivations of the instructor, for these individuals such behavior will detract from the enjoyment of the scuba experience.

In contrast, you may also find that some students have learned to be dependent on others to do things that they could do themselves. Again, this learned dependence may well stem from people around this individual attempting to protect them or simply to make their life easier. These students may be comfortable with an instructor who is a "Mother Hen." They might even expect it. However, once again, such behavior may detract from the quality of the instruction as well as the scuba experience itself.

Ultimately, it is the student who should determine how far she will progress in scuba. However, by your approach, you can play a role in helping the student to develop to her maximum potential. On the other hand, even with the best of intentions, you can inadvertently limit the student's opportunities for development and accomplishment as a scuba diver. As an instructor, you must set realistic and reasonable goals for the student based on an honest assessment of that student's abilities and desires. By assisting the student to realize her maximum potential, you will play an important role in "self-actualization", a process in which the student develops positive feelings about herself as well as about physical activity.

SCHEDULING YOUR CLASSES

When planning an Adapted Scuba Course, it is important that you build a great deal of flexibility into the time schedule. Some students with physical disabilities will require extra time to change their clothing, move back and forth from the locker room to the pool, or to assemble or disassemble their equipment. In some cases, this may simply mean that they, and probably you, must plan on arriving early and staying late. However, in those instances where access to a facility is strictly limited, extra class sessions may be required.

Locking your students into a rigid schedule for skills training may also be impractical. As is true with their able-bodied counterparts, students with disabilities will vary in their rate of learning. However, when working with individuals with disabilities, it may take extra time to determine a technique which is most effective for them. This may actually be more difficult for you than for the student. Remember that for the student this process of trial and error may well be a fact of daily life and you may benefit from their experience and creativity. It is very possible that they will help you develop techniques which are also easy for all of your students to use. By carefully reviewing the student's medical history and discussing the situation with the prospective student, you should develop an overall awareness of the student's disability or special needs. This will make it easier for you to anticipate any adaptations or accommodations which may be necessary.

SITE SELECTION

Difficulties can also arise when considering dive sites and activities for open water training. Unfortunately, many beaches and dive boats are not easily accessible for divers with disabilities. The instructor must be creative in conducting open water training so that each and every student receives the best possible open water experience. To achieve this goal, the instructor should be prepared to put in extra time and make extra dives as necessary. For example, it may be that only one of your local dive sites is easily accessible for divers who use wheelchairs. As the instructor, you must decide if you will conduct all training dives for the entire class at this one site. This decision will involve consideration of the benefits of diving other sites versus the logistics of accessing the other sites. Typically, with a little ingenuity and advance planning, issues such as these can be resolved and all class members can enjoy a variety of dive sites. However, everyone is better off if you consider these issues before you choose the dive site.

When selecting dive sites for your program, you must consider all of the typical factors such as parking, rest room facilities, proximity to restaurants, beach access, considerations for entering and exiting the water, and access to the local emergency medical system. However, for some divers with disabilities, any of these factors may assume more importance than usual. For instance, depending on the needs of the student, access to toilet facilities may be extremely important. In other cases, protection from sun, wind or cold may be extremely important, especially when spending a full day on the beach or dive boat. The student should be aware of his needs, but it will be up to you to make sure that he understands what to expect as far as environmental conditions, facilities, and time frames. This will assist the student in letting you know about any special concerns he may have and how you can assist in accommodating these concerns.

The following is a list of some common concerns and practical solutions to them.

Parking
Issues

Vans equipped with lifts may require more parking space than other vehicles. Is there adequate parking?

Solution

An easy option is selecting dive sites with adequate handicapped parking. However this assumes that such dive sites are available. Other options include arriving early to ensure your choice of appropriate spaces and carpooling to minimize the number of parking spaces needed.

Shelter

Issues

Exposure to sun, heat, cold, or wind for long periods of time can pose serious hazards to some individuals with disabilities.

Solution

Select dive sites with adequate shelter which is accessible to individuals who use wheelchairs or who have impaired mobility. Another option is to carry tents, awnings or other forms of shelter which are easily erected to provide protection from the elements. Getting into a vehicle is another simple option. However, this means that the vehicle must be reasonably close to the dive site. Also make sure that there is plenty of drinking water, sunscreen, and warm dry clothing available to your all students. On hot days, be prepared to dowse your students with water to help them stay cool.

Facilities

Issues

Access to facilities for toilets, changing clothing, and other private matters may be of concern for some divers.

Solution

Once again, if they are available, the easy option is to select dive sites with facilities which are accessible to people who use wheelchairs or who have impaired mobility. However, in the absence of such facilities you can use tents, awnings or other temporary shelters. A group of divers holding towels or blankets can be very effective and is something even a dive instructor's budget can handle. Portable receptacles can be used to collect waste.

Access

Issues

Ideally, divers who use wheel chairs should never have to leave their wheelchairs or require more than usual assistance when moving to and from the dive site. Unfortunately, the number of such dive sites available to you and your students may be very limited. Barriers which are commonly encountered at dive sites include: fences, walls, narrow gates, stairs, soft ground, sand, rocks, hills, steep slopes and ramps, and even excessively high curbs.

Solution

Evaluate the site for access prior to arriving with the class. This calls for some advance scouting with someone who uses a wheelchair. If you want a real challenge, put yourself in a wheelchair and see how accessible the beach is to you. Don't forget to consider that many students may be tired after a day of diving and this may have an impact on their ability to negotiate obstacles which were not a problem earlier in the day.

Soft Ground

Issues

Perhaps the most common barrier when beach diving is sand or soft ground which can be extremely difficult to traverse.

Solution

Fortunately, there are a number of simple solutions to make crossing soft ground easier on everyone. Placing a material on the ground in front of a wheelchair can prevent it from sinking in and make it much easier to wheel across soft ground. The same techniques may also make it easier for divers with impaired mobility to walk across soft ground. Examples of such materials include plastic fencing used to control snow or soil erosion, plywood strips, canvas, and tarpaulins. Typically, these are easily found at a local hardware store. A friend of mine even swears that just placing dried kelp in front of his chair gives him better purchase and makes beach crossings much easier.

In some cases you may wish to go so far as to build walkways or ramps. If so, make sure that they are sturdy enough to hold the weight of a person in a wheelchair and that they are securely anchored so they won't shift. It may also be advisable to include guard rails to prevent chairs from slipping off the side. When building ramps, the slope should be no more than 1" change in height for every 12" of horizontal distance covered.

CHAPTER SUMMARY

Developing a successful program which includes students both with and without special needs requires successfully meshing a number of different factors. Finding students, developing a staff, selecting training facilities and open water training sites, and establishing a workable schedule all require time and energy. Developing skills and knowledge in these areas will make life much easier for you. Fortunately, a variety of resources are available so you don't have to reinvent the wheel. These resources include professionals and organizations in your local community as well as in the scuba community. As an instructor, you should stay current with the resources out there. You should also be prepared to make your contribution to the body of knowledge that is being developed by those of us actively promoting scuba for people with special needs. By doing so, you increase the likelihood of success, not just for you and your programs, but for all programs which make scuba available to anyone who wishes to participate.

REVIEW OF MAIN POINTS

- Many of the concerns of a student with a disability or special needs are the same as any other student.
- Professionals in fields such as recreation, rehabilitation, or physical therapy may not be aware of the benefits scuba diving offers their clients. They may even resist their client's efforts to enroll in your class. Be prepared to educate these individuals and recruit them to work with you.
- Don't rush out and recruit large numbers of divers with special needs to enroll in your program. Start slowly and develop your knowledge, skills and comfort.

- It may be advisable to conduct the first training session as a one-on-one between you and the student. This session will allow you and the student to anticipate any special needs and determine how to accommodate them.
- Avoid stereotyping people. Remember that just because someone is said to "have a disability" does not mean that "they are disabled".
- The size of your staff should be determined by the size of the class and the needs of the students.
- Special training for your staff may not be necessary, but it is certainly an asset.
- Enlist divers with disabilities to assist you in teaching your classes.
- Be aware of how staff time is allocated and encourage cooperation between all members of the class.
- Avoid being a "Mother Hen." Assist your students in setting goals which are realistic and challenging, then assist them in attaining those goals.
- Self-actualization is a process in which a person develops positive feelings about themselves as well as physical activity.
- Allow plenty of flexibility in the class schedule.
- Conduct scouting missions to assess potential training sites for barriers.
- Inform students in advance of anticipated environmental conditions, and be prepared to assist them in protecting themselves from harsh conditions.

REVIEW QUESTIONS

1. Outline your own personal philosophy and guidelines for how you will structure your course and who you would like to see participate. Consider factors such as student mix, staff ratios, and your personal goals and objectives.
2. Identify some sources for finding students for your program and describe where these sources might be found. Now contact those sources you have actually found within your community.
3. Discuss important aspects of staff training and outline a program for training your staff.

4. Explain the concepts of learned dependence and self-actualization. Discuss how they might impact you in your role as a scuba instructor.
5. Discuss how including divers with special needs might impact your class schedule, and outline schedules appropriate for your program.
6. Evaluate local open water training sites for parking, shelter, facilities, access, and soft ground. Identify which sites are appropriate for your program and develop plans for open water training dives.

REFERENCES

Emmerson, L., Ravendale, J., Atterbury, S., Isabelle, H., North York Y-Nauts, Toronto Snorkelauts, Carmichael, B., Garrett, G., & Murray, R.. (n.d.). Skin diving for the physically handicapped. (Available from Moray Wheels Adaptive Scuba Association, PO Box 1660 GMF, Boston, MA. 02205)

Morrison, H. & Sinclair, S. (1987). Diving for those with disabilities: A guide for scuba diving instructors. Australian Underwater Federation National Headquarters, P.O. Box 1006, Civic Square A.C.T. 2608 Australia

National Oceanic and Atmospheric Administration (1991). Diving with disabilities. In NOAA diving manual diving for science and technology (pp. A1-A11). Silver Spring, MD: National Oceanic and Atmospheric Administration.

Open Waters (1994). Open waters scuba diving for everyone: A guide to making diving training accessible to people with disabilities. (Available from Open Waters c/o Alpha One, 127 Main St., South Portland, ME 04106)

Osinski, A. (1993). Modifying public swimming pools to comply with provisions of the americans with disabilities act. Palaestra, 9(4), 13-18.

Robinson, J., & Fox, A. D. (1987). Scuba diving with disabilities. Champaign, IL: Leisure Press.

Sherrill C. (1993). Adapted physical activity, recreation and sport: Crossdisciplinary and lifespan (4th ed.). WCB Brown & Benchmark: Dubuque.

Water Sports Division of the British Sports Association for the Disabled. (1983). Water sports for the disabled (pp. 112-126). West Yorkshire: EP Publishing Ltd.

Williamson, J. A., McDonald, R. W., Galligan, E. A., Baker, P.G., & Hammond, C. T. D (1984). Selection and training of disabled persons for scuba diving Medical and psychological aspects. The Medical Journal of Australia, 141, 414-418.

YMCA of the USA (1987). Aquatics for Special Populations. Champaign, IL: Human Kinetics.

RESOURCES FOR DEVELOPING AND PROMOTING AN ADAPTED SCUBA PROGRAM

- Check at the state, county, or city level for an Office of Therapeutic Services, Office of Special Education, or other similar programs.
- Programs for individuals with disabilities might also be offered through departments such as recreation, parks, or community services.
- Check at local universities, colleges, and junior colleges for programs such as Adapted Physical Education, Adapted Physical Activities, Occupational Therapy, Physical Therapy, Therapeutic Recreation, Recreation and Leisure Studies, or Disabled Student Services.
- Contact local hospitals for information regarding Occupational Rehabilitation Centers, Outpatient Centers, Independent Living Centers, or Physical Therapy Programs.
- Local community centers, recreation centers, YMCAs or health clubs may offer aquatic programs or other exercise programs for persons with disabilities.
- Inquire at the Chamber of Commerce or check the Yellow Pages for listings of Physical Therapists or rehabilitation/activity centers for individuals with disabilities.

RELATED CONCEPTS AND PROFESSIONS

Therapy	The treatment of disease, physical or mental disorder, or pathological condition.
Physical Therapy	The treatment of disease, injury, etc. by physical means such as heat, ice, massage or exercise.
Occupational Therapy	Therapy utilizing work and play, such as arts and crafts, to improve or restore functions impaired or lost through illness, injury or some other means. The goals of occupational therapy include enabling the client to live and function independently.

Therapeutic Recreation	The use of recreation services to change behavior or enhance growth and development in an individual.
Community Recreation	The use of community resources to enhance leisure time, improve quality of life and promote self-actualization.
Adapted Physical Education	The body of knowledge that identifies the special physical needs of an individual and provides educational opportunities which accommodate those needs.
Adapted Scuba	Recreational scuba training which accommodates the abilities and needs of individuals with disabilities.
Adaptive	The term adaptive refers to behavior and the ability to adapt.

ACTIVE ADAPTED SCUBA GROUPS
Training Organizations and Clubs

American Association of Challenged
Divers
John Ellerbock
P.O. Box 501405
San Diego, CA 95120-1045

619/597-8978

Dis-A-Dive
Bart Schasfoort
1250 Old river Rd.,
Cleveland, OH 44113-1222

216/752-3483

Divers Unlimbited
Teage Cadez
724 Loranne Ave.,
Pomona, CA

909/629-0832

Eels on Wheels Adaptive Scuba Club
Scott Ogren
1126 Corona Dr.,
Austin, TX 78723

512/335-5227

Handicapped Scuba Association
Jim Gatacre
1104 El Prado,
San Clemente, CA 92672

714/498-6128

Houston Disabled Scuba Divers Association
Lenny Hulsebosuh
150 Dominion Park Dr. 404,
Houston, TX 77090

713/873-4027

Moray Wheels: Adaptive Scuba Asso-
ciation
Rusty Murray
P.O. Box 1660 GMF,
Boston, MA 02205

603/598-4292

National Instructors Association for   408/379-6536
Divers with Disabilities
Dorothy Shrout & Frank Degnan
P.O. Box 112223,
Campbell, CA 95011

Open Waters   800/640-7200
c/o Alpha One
Steve Tremblay & Paul Rollins
127 Main Street,
South Portland, ME 04106

Petrofsky Center   714/855-4837
Dr. Joseph Petrofsky
13765 Alton Parkway #E,
Irvine, CA 92718

Scuba Ventures Inc.   205/870-0203
Mark Digorgio
P.O. Box 360034,
Birmingham, AL 35236

Zero Gravity   207/773-3483
Bill Demmons
P.O. Box 2893,
South Portland, ME 04116

Resorts

Divi Flamingo Beach Resort and Casino   800/367-3484
Divi Hotels Marketing Inc.
2401 N.W. 34th Ave. Miami, FL 33142

Kosrae Village Resort Kosrae,   691/370-5165
FSM, Kosrae, 96944
(This resort is located in the Federated States of Micronesia.)

Red Sail Sports   800/255-6425
Programs are offered in Aruba and Grand Cayman

GENERAL PRODUCTS FOR INDIVIDU-ALS WITH SPECIAL NEEDS

adaptAbility   800/288-9941
PO Box, Colchester, CT 06415-0515

Danmar Products Inc.   800/783-1998
221 Jackson Industrial Dr., Ann Arbor, MI 48103

SEATCASE, Inc.   (800) 221-SEAT
6108 Dedham Lane, Austin, TX 78739

Urocare Products Inc.   (800) 423-4441
2735 Melbourne Ave., Pomona, CA 91767

RESOURCES FOR POOL ACCESS DEVICES

AFW Co. of North America   (716) 372-2935
P.O. Box 648, Cohoes, NY 12047

Aquatic Access Inc.   (502) 425-5817
417 Dorsey Way, Louisville, KY 40223   (800) 325-LIFT

Hoyer Operations   (414) 236-3460
2815 Oregon St., Oshkosh, WI 54901

Lincoln Equipment, Inc.   (714) 990-6015
182 Viking Ave., Brea, CA 92821

Recreonics   (317) 872-4400
4200 Schmitt Ave., Louisville, KY 40213   (800) 428-3254

Rehab Systems   (701) 293-9175
1720 3rd Ave. North, Fargo, ND 58102   (800) 726-8620

Recreation Supply Co.   (800) 437-8072
P.O. Box 2757, Bismark, ND 58502

Swim-Lifts; Spectrum Pool Products   (406) 543-5309
7100 Spectrum Ln., Missoula, MT 59802

Triad Technologies   (315) 437-4089
219 Lamson St., Syracuse, NY 13206

United Industries Swim Time   (800) 835-3272
202 E. Cleveland St., Sterling, KS 67579

Glossary

A

Americans with Disabilities Act
Legislation enacted in 1990 intended to ensure that individuals with disabilities enjoy full and equal access to public facilities.

adapted physical education
The body of knowledge that identifies the special physical needs of an individual and provides educational opportunities which accommodate those needs.

adapted scuba instruction
Scuba instruction programs which encourage participation by individuals with disabilities or special needs.

adaptive
The term adaptive refers to behavior and the ability to adapt.

aisle chairs
Narrow wheelchairs designed to fit in the aisles of airplanes.

amputation
Absence of a limb or part of a limb.

anti-tip casters
Small wheels at the rear of a wheelchair which prevent the chair from tipping over backwards.

assistive devices
Devices which help an individual to perform tasks such as walking, grabbing or holding.

athetosis
Slow, uncontrolled movements.

autonomic dysreflexia
A life threatening situation created when spinal cord damage blocks the body's attempts to notify the brain about some undesirable stimulus.

B

butt walk
A form of locomotion in which the person sits on the ground facing away from the desired direction of travel, and then uses her upper body to drag or scoot her body backwards.

C

camber
The angle of the wheels on a wheelchair.

casters
Small forward wheels of a wheelchair.

cauda equina
Portion of the spinal cord known as the "horses tail".

cerebral palsy
A neurologic disorder affecting both posture and movement.

cervical vertebrae
The seven vertebrae located in the neck region of the body.

changing tables
Padded tables on which individuals can lie while changing clothes.

coccyx
The vertebrae immediately below the sacrum. Also known as the tailbone.

colostomy
Surgical procedure to create a stoma to allow for the collection of solid waste.

community recreation
The use of community resources to enhance leisure time, improve quality of life and promote self-actualization.

complete spinal cord injury
An injury resulting in complete loss of both sensation and voluntary control of body functions controlled by nerves which exit the spine below the level of injury.

congenital amputation
An amputation present at birth.

D
decubiti
Ulcers or pressure sores caused by bone pressing against skin.

depressing
Procedure in which individuals who use wheelchairs relieve pressure on their skin by shifting in their seats or lifting themselves up.

dill stick
A device used to manually extract solid waste form the body.

E
etiquette
Using proper language and offering assistance in a constructive manner, to create an atmosphere of comfort for individuals with disabilities.

everyday wheelchair
Light-weight wheelchair used by athletes and individuals capable of pushing themselves.

external plumbing
A urine collection system consisting of an external catheter, tube and collection bag worn on the leg.

F
foot fall
A situation where the foot of an individual using a wheelchair falls off the footrest.

G
gusset
Material added to a garment to make it roomier.

I
ileostomy
Surgical procedure to create a stoma to allow for the collection of solid waste.

incomplete spinal cord injury
An injury resulting in partial loss or sensation or control of body functions controlled by nerves which exit the spine below the level of injury.

internal catheterization
Inserting a catheter into the urethra and draining urine into a disposable container.

involvement
This term refers to any body parts which have been affected by spinal cord injury.

L
lesions
Injuries to the spine.

lumbar vertebrae
The five vertebrae located in the lower back region of the body.

M

medical model wheelchair
Wheelchair typically found in health care institutions and other large facilities.

motorized wheelchair
Self propelled wheelchair powered by a battery.

O

occupational therapy
Therapy utilizing work and play, such as arts and crafts, to improve or restore functions impaired or lost through illness, injury or some other means. The goals of occupational therapy include enabling the client to live and function independently.

orthopedic disability
Injuries involving deformities, injuries and diseases of the bones, joints, and muscles.

osteoporosis
Loss of calcium in bone tissue causing the bone to become brittle and more susceptible to fracture.

orthoses
Devices, such as braces and splints, used to correct a deformity, improve function or provide support to prevent collapse.

P

paralysis
A condition in which voluntary control of muscle function is lost. However depending on the nature of the injury, involuntary movements such as muscle spasms may occur. Paralysis may be complete meaning that all voluntary control is lost, or partial/incomplete, meaning some control has been retained.

paraplegia
A condition in which both of the lower limbs are involved to some extent. Trunk balance may also be involved.

paresis
Muscle weakness associated with partial paralysis.

pedestals
Alternate name for footrests on a wheelchair.

person-first terminology
Language which places the individual ahead of the disability.

phantom limb
A phenomenon in which some individuals with amputations experience sensations such as itching or pain as if the limb is still present.

physical disability
Any physical condition which compromises a diver's safety or ability to perform standard scuba skills. In some cases, specific legal or medical criteria may apply.

physical therapy
The treatment of disease, injury, etc. by physical means such as heat, ice, massage or exercise.

poikilothermy
Difficulty regulating body temperature.

power wheelchair
Self propelled wheelchair powered by a battery.

prostheses
Refers to a device used to replace or substitute for a missing limb.

Q
quadriplegia
A condition in which all four of the limbs and the trunk are involved to some extent.

A Guide for Teaching Scuba to Divers with Special Needs

R

roll bar
A bar placed behind the front of the frame of a sport chair, to prevent the frame from gouging the floor.

S

sacrum
The vertebrae immediately below the lumbar vertebrae.

self-actualization
The process by which you develop positive feelings about yourself and about physical activity.

self-concept
The perception you have of yourself based on your feelings, opinions and beliefs about yourself.

sliding board
A board used to bridge the gap when transferring between two objects of the same height.

spasticity
Excessive muscle tightness and stiffness.

special physical needs
Needs unique to a diver which cause the diver to require special equipment, training accommodations or assistance to perform skills typical of recreational scuba.

spinal cord
A bundle of nerve fibers which allow nerve impulses to be sent between the body and the brain.

spinal cord injury
Neurological deficit resulting from bruising, crushing, severing, or hemorrhaging of the spine.

sport wheelchair
Lightweight wheelchair used by wheelchair athletes.

stoma
A surgically created opening between a body cavity and the surface of the body.

stump
The end of a limb which has been amputated.

T

therapeutic recreation
The use of recreation services to change behavior or enhance growth and development in an individual.

therapy
The treatment of disease, physical or mental disorder, or pathological condition.

thoracic vertebrae
The vertebrae located in the thoracic, or chest area, of the body.

tipping lever
Lever which protrudes from the rear of a wheelchair and is used by an assistant to tip the chair backwards.

traditional scuba training
A training process which seeks to produce divers who are capable of acting independently at all times, whether in or out of the water.

transfer
Term referring to techniques used to move from one position to another such as from a wheelchair to the ground.

transfer board
A board used to bridge the gap when transferring between two objects of the same height.

U
upper body swimmer
A diver who is not able to kick and so must swim using the upper body.

V
vertebrae
Individual bones protecting the spinal cord. Together the vertebrae form the spinal or vertebral column.

vital capacity
The maximum amount of air that can be exhaled following the deepest possible inhalation.

Index

---

sensation, 3-8, 4-43, 4-48, 5-2
shelter, 7-7, 7-10
shelters, 6-5, 7-7
site selection, 7-6
sliding board, 5-10
snorkels, 3-1, 3-2, 3-10, 3-11
sores, 2-7
spasms, 2-6, 2-11, 2-13, 5-2
spasticity, 2-13
special education, 7-12
special physical needs, I-1,
    I-2, 7-13
spinal cord, I-1, 2-3, 3-12,
    4-65
    cervical, 2-4
    lumbar, 2-4
    sacrum, 2-3
    Thoracic, 2-4
spinal cord injury, I-1, 2-3,
    3-12, 4-65
staff training, 7-3
stoma, 2-8
stump, 3-6, 3-11

–T–
cylinders, 3-8, 3-9, 3-11
telephone, 6-2
temperature, 2-5, 3-7, 6-3
terminology, 1-2
Therapeutic Recreation, 7-12,
    7-13
Therapeutic Services, 7-12
therapy, 7-12, 7-13
    Occupational Therapy,
        7-12
    Therapeutic Recreation,
        7-12
    Therapeutic Services, 7-12
thermoregulation, 2-10

tissue breakdown, 2-7
toilet, 6-2, 7-6
traditional scuba training, I-2
transfer, 2-11, 4-13, 4-14, 5-9,
    5-10, 5-14, 5-16, 5-17, 5-18,
    5-19, 5-20, 6-4
    transfer board, 5-10
    transfers, 4-20, 4-30, 5-9,
        5-18, 5-19, 5-20
travel, 2-19

–U–
ulcers, 2-7

–V–
vertebrae, 2-3
    cervical, 2-4
    lumbar, 2-4
    sacrum, 2-3
    thoracic, 2-4
voluntary movement, 4-11,
    4-13

–W–
walkways, 6-2, 6-3, 7-8
weight belts, 3-4, 3-5, 4-50
    weight integrated, 3-4
    weight systems, 3-5, 3-11
weighting, 4-49
weights, 2-14, 3-4, 3-5, 4-23,
    4-49, 4-50, 4-51, 4-53, 4-57,
    4-59, 4-60
wetsuits, 3-7, 4-13, 5-14
wheelchair, 2-11, 4-30, 5-1,
    5-3, 5-9, 5-14, 5-18, 5-19,
    5-20, 6-1, 6-2, 6-4, 6-5, 7-8
    aisle chairs, 2-20
    chairs, 2-20